Gifts for Bird Lovers

Over 50 Projects to Make and Give

ALTHEA L. SEXTON

A Storey Publishing Book

STOREY

STOREY COMMUNICATIONS, INC.
SCHOOLHOUSE ROAD
POWNAL, VERMONT 05261

The mission of Storey Communications is to serve our customers by publishing practical information that encourages personal independence in harmony with the environment.

Edited by Brooke Dyer-Bennet and Deborah Balmuth
Designed by Meredith Maker
Text production by Eugenie S. Delaney
Production assistance by Erin Lincourt and Leslie Noyes
Cover and finished project illustration by Frank Riccio
Instructional drawings by Brigita Fuhrmann
Indexed by Northwind Editorial Services

Projects on the following pages are excerpted or adapted from previously published Storey books:

page 14 from *Herbal Treasures;* pages 21 and 53 from *Backyard Bird Lovers Guide;* pages 33, 65, 71, 73, and 78 from *Everything You Never Learned about Birds;* and page 90 from *Making Your Own Paper.*

Storey Publishing books are available for special premium and promotional uses and for customized editions. For further information, please call the Custom Publishing Department at 1-800-793-9396.

Printed in the United States by R. R. Donnelley
10 9 8 7 6 5 4 3 2 1

Library of Congress Cataloging-in-Publication Data

Sexton, Althea L., 1962-
  Gifts for bird lovers: over 50 projects to make and give / Althea L. Sexton.
        p.   cm.
  Includes bibliographical references (p.   ) and index.
  ISBN 0-88266-981-8 (pbk. : alk. paper)
    1. Handicraft. 2. Gifts. 3. Birds in art. 4. Bird watchers-
-Miscellanea. I. Title.
TT157.S4164   1997
745.5—dc21   97-14569
                                                      CIP

CONTENTS

INTRODUCTION

Almost everyone has a bird story to tell. Mine is about the bald eagle I saw on the Washington coast a few years ago. The weather had been cooperative that day. The sun was shining — a rare occurrence in some parts of the Pacific Northwest. We had walked a couple of miles up the beach, then turned back as the sun began to set. Someone in the group commented that all we needed now was to see one of the eagles that nested in the area.

No sooner were the words out of her mouth than an eagle flew over, just a hundred feet above our heads. The bird was beautiful, and it seemed to fly in slow motion. That lone bird completed a perfect day.

When I opened my window shades this morning, I saw birds at the feeder. I'd seen birds there before, of course, but never really noticed them. This time I became excited as I recognized the species from research for this book. It occurred to me that I was in danger of becoming a bird watcher — an affliction affecting millions around the world. Birders can be recognized by the faraway look in their eyes. A field guide is usually stuffed into one of their pockets. Their binoculars and notebooks confirm the diagnosis.

Bird lovers are a fascinating breed. Dedicated and tenacious, they scan hedgerows, the tree lines, and roadsides in their never-ending search for another species to add to their tally. In their enthusiasm for birds, they are in the forefront of habitat preservation. This, in turn, serves all of us who love wildlife.

Bird-watching is a multimillion-dollar industry, and still growing. The U.S. Fish and Wildlife Service estimates that 63 million Americans spend about two billion dollars a year on bird feed. Bird-watching is becoming more popular as people discover its benefits.

In this book, you will find many easy-to-make projects for the bird lover in your life. Many of the designs are adaptable to more than one project. Be creative and experiment with all of them. And don't forget to feed the birds.

ACKNOWLEDGMENTS

No book is ever written without the help of many people. To the writers on listserv, RW-l, I can never say thank you enough for your friendship and support. I'm grateful for the willingness of the folks at newsgroup, rec.birds to answer questions about odd things. To my friends, Jennifer Strait, Patty Fischer, and Joanne Delazzari; who have encouraged me to write, many thanks and the coffee's on. To Deborah Balmuth, who gave me this opportunity, I bow in your general direction. And to Brooke Dyer-Bennet, I hope the manuscript wasn't too hopeless.

To my children, Alexander and Meghan,

who are as much a labor of love

as is this bit of printed word.

CHAPTER 1

Gifts for Bird Watchers

At the close of the day when the hamlet is still,

And mortals the sweets of forgetfulness prove,

When naught but the torrent is heard on the hill,

And naught but the nightingale's song in the grove.

— James Beattie (1735–1803), "The Hermit"

Choosing gifts can often be a study in frustration. If you have bird lovers on your list, look inside this chapter and the rest of the book for many beautiful and useful projects.

When you make the gift yourself, you tell the recipient how much you care. The projects in this chapter will help any bird watcher in the hobby they enjoy.

Birding Notebook

A birding notebook is an essential — and much cherished — tool. Within its pages the birder records all of her significant sightings. Personalize this gift by using a map of your birder's region; a shorebird design if the birder lives on a coast; a loon, perhaps, for someone who does her bird-watching near a lake.

MATERIALS

6 sheets of paper, 8½″ x 11″
   or 4¼″ x 5½″
1 sheet cover stock, 8¾″ x 11¼″
   or 4½″ x 5¾″
Stout thread, 22″
Stencil Mylar
Acrylic or stencil paint

EQUIPMENT

Ruler
Scissors
X-acto knife
Stencil brush or small sponge

1 Make a stencil (see page 103 for technique), using the feather pattern on page 108, or another design of your choice.

2 Measure the cover paper and with a pencil draw a light line down the center. This will give you the location of the spine of your notebook. Decorate the front cover by placing the stencil on the right side of the pencil line and painting it. Allow to dry. Fold in half along the pencil line.

3 Fold the sheets of paper in half to the dimensions, either 4¼″ x 5½″ or 2⅛″ x 2¾″. Place them inside one another and then inside the cover sheet.

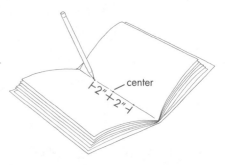

4 With the pencil, make a small mark at the center and at 2″ both above and below the first mark. You should have four roughly equal divisions. Make holes at these three marks. Hold the papers in place with binder clips if necessary.

5 Thread the needle. Double the thread and knot, leaving a 2″ tail to make a finishing bow after sewing the booklet together.

6 Working from the inside of the booklet, push the needle down. Come back up through the top hole. Go through the middle hole again and come back up in the bottom hole. Tie off.

DECORATING THE COVER

You can use a variety of decorations on the front of the birding notebook:

∾ Stencil the picture of the bird in metallic paint.

∾ Use a feather to stamp the front cover.

∾ Make the cover of plain handmade paper, or add bits of feather to the mix.

∾ Photocopy a picture of a bird on heavy cover stock for a realistic image. Color it with pencils or watercolor paints.

VARIATIONS

∾ Nature print with a feather on each page (see pages 70–71 for technique).

∾ Use a metallic cord instead of stout thread. Finish with a bow or tassel.

∾ Preprint the paper with a bird-watching form.

Bird-Watching Form ∾

Date _____ Time _____
Location _____
Species _____ # _____
Sex/ Age _____
Body (size, shape, color, wings, tail)
_____
_____
_____

Head and bill (size, shape, color)
_____
_____
_____

Legs and feet (size, length, color)
_____
_____
_____

In flight (profile, color, wing/tail, wing beats)
_____
_____
_____

Voice _____
_____
_____

Behavior _____
_____
_____

Habitat _____
_____
_____

Birding Hat

Every dedicated birder needs a good hat to keep out the rain, as well as to shield him or her from harsh rays of sun. Make this one out of heavy canvas or waterproof fabric to keep the head dry and warm. Decorate the hat with bands of fabric or ribbon tied around the crown.

MATERIALS

Paper for pattern
⅝ yard fashion fabric, 45″ wide
1 yard fabric for lining
1⅛ yard fusible interfacing
1″ grosgrain ribbon, at least 24″ long

EQUIPMENT

Measuring tape
Scissors
Iron
Sewing machine
Needle and thread

Note: Seam allowances are ⅝″.

CUTTING

1 Enlarge patterns on page 108. You can use brown paper, recycled computer paper, or old newsprint.

To ensure that the size is right, measure the head around the crown. The measuring tape should be snug but not too tight. Adjust pattern according to crown measurement, either adding or taking away as needed.

Mark the quarter marks on the seam lines on the top, crown, and inner seam of the brim.

2 Cut pattern pieces out of fashion fabric. In addition, cut for the lining, 1 crown and 1 top; and for the interfacing, 1 of each piece. Transfer the quarter marks to the fabric pieces.

3 Fuse interfacing to the wrong side of the fashion fabric according to manufacturer's directions.

THE TOP

4 Place fashion fabric and lining wrong sides together, sandwiching the interfacing. Baste along outer edges ½″ in.

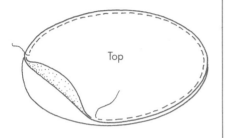

THE CROWN

5 Sew ends of crown together on both fashion fabric and lining. Trim seam allowances to ¼″ and press open.

6 Place the right side of the crown against the right side of the top with the crown seam at the mark in the back. Ease in fullness, matching the marks, and hand baste. Repeat steps 5 and 6 with the lining. Sew and trim the seam allowances.

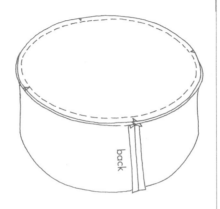

7 Place lining and fashion fabric top/crown constructions against each other, wrong sides facing, and baste the lower edges together.

8 Sew together the ends of both brim pieces. Trim the seam allowances and press open. Place the top and bottom pieces of the brim right sides together, matching the seams. Sew outer

edges, turn, and trim the seam allowances. Topstitch ⅛ inch from edge. Match the quarter points. Baste the inner edge.

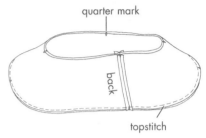

9 Pin the brim to the crown, matching the quarter points. Baste and sew, easing in fullness to the brim. Trim the seam allowance.

10 By hand, sew the ribbon over the seam allowance by whipstitching over the upper and lower edges. Fold ends under to finish.

Binoculars Strap and Cover

It seems that every bird watcher has a preference for a particular type of binoculars. This custom cross-stitched strap and cover will be perfect for any binoculars the birder nearest you chooses. It will keep a birder's most valuable piece of equipment safe from flying branches and out of rain.

MATERIALS

For the strap:

Aida cloth, 10 squares to the inch, 3"–4" wide x desired length of strap, plus 2" (approximately 36")

Embroidery floss or perle cotton:
  Off-white to work the background
  One color for working the birds
  One color for the edging
  Yellow for the beaks
  Black for eyes and outlining

Fusible interfacing, 1" wide x desired length of strap plus 2" (approximately 36")

½" grosgrain ribbon, length of strap (approximately 36")

2" of 1"-wide Velcro

For the cover:

Circle of waterproof fabric (size based on binoculars measurements), approximately 16"–18" in diameter

¼" elastic, approximately 16"–18" in diameter

1 spool of thread

Grosgrain ribbon, approximately 55"–60"

EQUIPMENT

Measuring tape
Scissors
Iron
Sewing machine

Take some measurements to ensure a good fit.

Binoculars strap: Drape measuring tape around neck, holding ends in one hand. Adjust until you feel comfortable with the length. Round up to the nearest whole number; otherwise you'll end up losing part of your cross-stitched bird. Add 2" to the length.

Binoculars cover: Measure around the binoculars at the widest point. Add 3" to get the diameter of the circle.

STRAP

1 Cut a piece of Aida cloth 3" wide and to the length of your strap measurement. Do the cross-stitch pattern. Use one color for the bird and another for the edging. Embellish the design with black French knots for eyes and yellow half-cross-stitches for the beaks. Repeat the motif the whole length of the strap, ending 1″ from the ends.

2 Cut a piece of interfacing to the width of the cross-stitch design. Turn the strap face down and fuse interfacing to the back of your needlework. This will cover the raw back of the handwork.

3 Fold edges of the needle-work over interfacing until the raw edges meet. You may need to trim the edges in order for them to butt up against each other. Whipstitch closed. Use a press cloth with your iron at a cotton setting. Turn ends of strap up 1″ and whip-stitch.

4 Place the grosgrain ribbon over the raw edges of the back. Using tiny stitches, sew in place down both sides of ribbon.

fold over end
whipstitch
interfacing

5 Sew Velcro on the strap ends so that one piece covers the end of the ribbon and the other is about 3″ up. They should both be on the same side of the strap as the ribbon. Hook the strap onto your birder's binoculars.

Cover

6 Cut circle large enough to form a bag that will completely cover binoculars. Fold edge under to wrong side ¼″ and press, being careful not to scorch the fabric.

7 To make a casing for elastic, place ribbon over the raw edge. Sew close to outer edge of

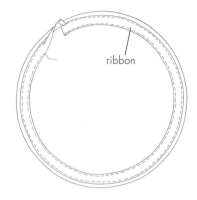

Velcro
ribbon
Velcro

waterproof cloth. Sew inner edge of grosgrain ribbon, leaving a 2″ opening to insert elastic.

ribbon

8 Measure the binoculars again and subtract 3″ to get the length for the elastic. Cut the elastic to the measured length.

9 Run elastic through the casing and sew the ends firmly together. Sew closed the opening in the casing.

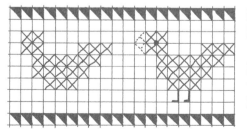

◣ Border — choice of color
◩ Bird body — choice of color
⠄ Beak — yellow
✦ Eye — black French knot
☐ Legs — black or choice of color

Sitting Pad

Make this item out of waterproof fabric for a gift any intrepid birder will love, especially on damp, chill mornings. Since keeping dry can mean the difference between a beautiful day and one filled with misery, protect your favorite birder with this sitting pad.

MATERIALS

2 pieces of waterproof fabric, 20″ square
Polyester quilt batting, 20″ square
2 pieces of fabric for ties, 2″ x 36″

EQUIPMENT

Straight pins
Sewing machine
Measuring tape
Needle and thread
Scissors

1 Place the fabric squares right sides together and put the batting on top. Pin and baste in place, stitching through all three layers. Run a basting stitch down the center of the sandwiched fabric in both directions to hold it in place while sewing the seams.

2 Fold the tie fabric in half lengthwise, right sides together. Sew along the edge, turn, and press. You will have two long tubes of fabric. Ends can be knotted to prevent fraying. Fold them in half.

3 On one edge, measure 6″ in from two corners of the square, pinning a tie at each of these spots so that the fold points to the outer edge. The long tails of the ties will be toward the center of the fabric squares. By hand, baste in place on the seam line.

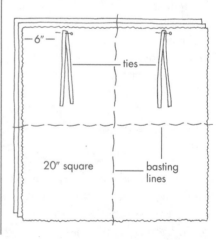

ties

6″

20″ square

basting lines

4 Starting at the side opposite the ties, sew around the edges of the fabric square, leaving a 3–4″ opening for turning the seat right side out.

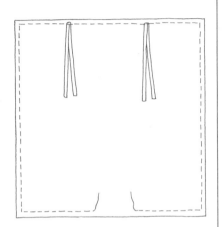

5 Reach in through the opening and grasp the ties; pull them to help turn the pad right side out. With your hands, flatten slightly.

6 Machine stitch or hand quilt lines 4″ apart. (This will keep the batting in place.) The pad can be rolled up and tied while not in use.

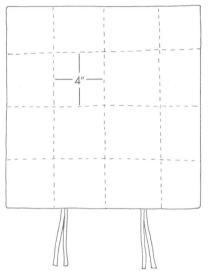

Birding Tips ✺

- ✺ Purchase a field guide to the birds native to your area. This will give you pictures and descriptions of the birds you are likely to see during local outings.
- ✺ Contact the state and national park services near you for a checklist of birds that visit your area.
- ✺ Check with the Audubon Society to learn of birding groups in your area. Local birders are an important resource when you are just beginning; they can point you in the right direction.
- ✺ Record any birds you see and identify in a notebook. This can be done by location and by season.
- ✺ When you are out in the field, please remember to respect the privacy and property of others, keep a good distance between you and any nesting sites, and stay on existing trails or roadways to avoid disturbing natural habitat.

Stamped Scarf

This cheerful, easy-to-make gift will help combat discomfort even on those cold days that deter all but the dedicated birder. Make it to give alone as a gift, or team it with one of the jewelry projects.

MATERIALS
Scarf
Freezer paper
Bird track stencil
Fabric paint

EQUIPMENT
Iron
Small stencil brush

1 Hand wash and dry the scarf to remove the sizing in the fabric. Iron flat. Cut a piece of freezer paper that is larger than the area to be stenciled. With the freezer paper shiny side up, place the area of the scarf that is to be stenciled on top of the paper. Iron. (The paper provides support for the fabric.)

2 Transfer the design to a piece of stencil Mylar and cut it out.

3 Stencil the bird tracks along the edge of the scarf using the fabric paint and a small stencil brush (see page 103 for stenciling instructions).

4 Fix the paint according to manufacturer's directions.

Bird Track Stencil

Walking Stick

Any bird lover who covers rough terrain will value this whimsical walking stick. Make it from a hardwood, such as oak or any fruitwood, and rub oil into it for a beautiful finish. Add hand-carved touches and semiprecious stones for a truly unique gift.

MATERIALS

1 stout straight limb, 4′ to 5′ long, 1″–2″ in diameter (it should have enough thickness at the top to allow for carving)

Danish oil or wax finish

EQUIPMENT

Knife for carving

Sandpaper, coarse, medium, and fine grit

Danish oil or wax finish

1 Remove side branches from the stick using the knife or a saw. Clean the bark from the stick. With the knife, smooth any sharp points or burrs.

2 Use a pencil to mark carving lines at the top. Use the chicken head design shown, or try an eagle, cardinal, or raven.

3 Carve the bird's head in the top of the walking stick. Smooth with sandpaper. You can also carve swirls and spirals that go the length of the stick.

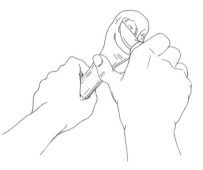

4 Apply the oil or wax finish according to the manufacturer's directions. Buff to a gloss with a clean, smooth cloth.

Add glass eyes to create a more realistic look. Semiprecious stones also make good eyes, and add an elegant touch. Hollow out a small space for them and use epoxy.

Warming Bag

This gift will keep someone on your gift list toasty warm. A couple of minutes in the microwave, and this rice-filled bag will retain heat for a long while. If you don't have a microwave, you can heat the raw rice in a skillet (make sure not to scorch it), and pour it carefully into the warming bag. Tuck the bag under a blanket to warm hands or feet.

MATERIALS

New athletic tube sock or fleece
  fabric, 8″ x 16″
3–4 cups uncooked rice
2 pieces of ribbon, each 18″ long
Needle and thread
Sewing machine, if using fleece

1 *If you're using a sock:* Cut the toe off the sock. Wrap one ribbon around the sock about 2″ from one end. Tie with a square knot, then make a bow. Fill the sock with rice and use the second ribbon to tie the opening closed 2″ in from the end.

2 *If you're using fleece:* Fold the fabric in half lengthwise with the right sides together. Pin or baste along the seam line. Sew the long edge with a straight stitch. Turn the tube right side out. Tie one end closed with a ribbon as in step 1. Fill the tube with rice and tie the open end closed with the second ribbon.

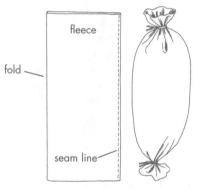

3 *To warm:* Microwave for 1–2 minutes and then as necessary to keep warm.

Potions to Pamper

After a long day of tramping about searching for feathered beauties, a long soak and a little TLC are called for. Essential oils make these potions good for the skin at the same time that they refresh the soul. Tuck them in a basket for a perfect gift.

Honey Lip Balm

2 tablespoons clarified honey
2 teaspoons aloe vera gel
10 drops chamomile essential oil
10 drops geranium essential oil
5 drops lemon essential oil
2 drops lavender essential oil

Mix all ingredients well, and store in an airtight container. Rub on chapped lips for soothing relief.

Luxurious Hand Lotion

1 ounce cocoa butter
1 ounce beeswax
3 tablespoons sweet almond oil
12 drops evening primrose oil
12 drops carrot oil

Add one of the following:
15 drops rose essential oil
15 drops neroli essential oil
or
15 drops sandalwood essential oil

In a double boiler, melt the cocoa butter and beeswax. Slowly add the sweet almond, evening primrose, and carrot oils. Let cool slightly and add the essential oil of your choice. Store in a dark container. Rub into your hands for soft skin.

Better-than-a-European-Spa Bath Oil

¼ cup sweet almond oil
¼ cup apricot kernel oil
2 tablespoons jojoba oil
20 drops jasmine essential oil
20 drops sandalwood essential oil
20 drops nutmeg essential oil

Mix all ingredients together and store in a decorative bottle. Add to bath a teaspoon at a time.

After-Bath Splash

10 drops orange essential oil
5 drops lemon essential oil
5 drops geranium essential oil
2 cups distilled vinegar
4 ounces cider vinegar
2 cups distilled water

Mix the essential oils together in a bottle, and add the vinegar. (You can use white wine vinegar, if you like.) Close the bottle and shake well. Let stand overnight. Add the water and shake well. Splash on after your bath for a soothing end to your pampering.

Herbal Insect Repellent

With the concern over chemicals in our lives, these recipes for safe and natural herbal lotions will be greatly appreciated.

Bug-Away Oil

⅛ ounce citronella
⅛ ounce patchouli
⅛ ounce vetiver essential oil
3 ounces sweet almond oil

Mix ingredients together and keep in a dark glass bottle.

Bug-Off Oil

12 drops eucalyptus essential oil
6 drops peppermint essential oil
6 drops ti tree oil
2 ounces sweet almond oil
Vitamin E (as a preservative)

Mix ingredients together and keep in a dark glass bottle.

After-Sun Oil

Being a bird watcher means you go where the birds are, which puts you outside and at the mercy of the sun. This luxurious skin oil will help replace moisture and soften your skin.

10 drops lavender essential oil
10 drops chamomile essential oil
5 drops bergamot essential oil
10 drops geranium essential oil
2 ounces almond oil
2 tablespoons sesame oil
1 tablespoon jojoba oil
1 teaspoon evening primrose oil

Mix together in a glass bottle. Keep handy to use whenever your skin needs a lift. Shake well before each application.

Gift Idea ✑

Put these lotions in bottles tied with raffia bows and nestle a few in a basket. Use handmade paper to make gift tags explaining how to use them.

CHAPTER 2

Gifts for the Gourmand Bird

*I*n the desert a fountain is springing,

In the wide waste there still is a tree,

And a bird in the solitude singing,

Which speaks to my spirit of thee.

— William Wordsworth (1770–1850), "Stanzas to Augusta"

Birdseed Mixes

Most commercial seed mixes contain a high percentage of cereals and filler. These are wasted because birds will kick them out of the feeder to get at their favorite seeds. You can save money and provide a better quality mix by buying seeds in bulk from a livestock feed store and blending them yourself. Avoid using whole corn, oats, buckwheat, wheat, rape seed, flax seed, and canary seed. Also bypass the artificial "berry-flavored" pellets and seeds colored to look like fruit; birds are too smart to fall for them. By using seeds that target specific birds, you can attract your favorites to your feeder. To broaden the variety of birds you feed, vary the mix. The chart will help you select a useful blend. You can't go wrong if you start with black oil sunflower seeds. These seeds are favored by a range of birds. The simplest mix is equal parts of black oil sunflower and thistle seed.

Seeds and Corn
This combination will appeal to many types of birds.

3 parts sunflower seed
3 parts millet
1 part finely cracked corn
3 parts hemp seed
1 part canary seed
Grit, free of contaminants such as
   oil or road salt

Mix together and use in any type of feeder.

Sunflower and Corn
Combine equal quantities of black oil sunflower seed and cracked corn. You can use this in elevated or ground-level feeders, but place the feeder near shrubbery — birds feel safer with cover nearby.

Fruit Candy
1/2 cup green grapes
1/2 cup blueberries
1 cup breadcrumbs
1 cup sunflower hearts
1 cup cracked corn
2 pounds suet
sprinkle of sand

Mix fruit, crumbs, and seeds in a foil lined pie pan. Melt the suet over low heat, allow to cool and re-melt. Let cool slightly and pour over other ingredients. Stir sand into the mixture and allow to cool completely. Remove from pan and break into pieces. Serve in ground feeder

Fruit Salad Plate
Mix together chopped apple, banana pieces, raisins, and cherries. Tear several slices of white bread into small pieces. Toss lightly with a 1/4 cup of sugar. Serve in ground feeder.

Bird Feed and Feeder Types ∾

FEED	FEEDER TYPE	BIRDS ATTRACTED
Black oil sunflower	Tube and house-type feeders	Cardinals, mountain chickadees, goldfinches, nuthatches, redpolls, woodpeckers
Striped sunflower	Tube and house-type feeders	Jays, grosbeaks
White millet	Platform feeders	Doves, towhees, juncos
Safflower	Tube and house-type feeders	House finches, nuthatches
Peanuts, crushed	Tube, house-type, and platform feeders	Jays, common flickers, cardinals, grackles, titmice
Sunflower hearts	Tube and house-type feeders	Pine siskins, cardinals
Thistle	Tube feeders	Lesser goldfinches, pine siskins, house finches, doves, chickadees, song sparrows
Cracked corn	Platform feeders	Thrashers, quail, jays, juncos, doves, starlings, grackles
Fruit	(none needed)	Orioles, mockingbirds, tanagers, bluebirds, cardinals, jays, thrashers, cedar waxwings
Hanging suet	Suet holder	Woodpeckers, chickadees, kinglets, wrens, nuthatches, thrashers, cardinals
Peanut butter suet	Suet holder	Woodpeckers, juncos, thrashers, wrens, goldfinches, cardinals, jays, bluebirds

Suet Christmas Tree Ornaments

Bring the holidays outdoors and provide welcome winter food at the same time. These simple ornaments can be made quickly to replenish the supply as long as there are hungry birds. They also make quick and easy gifts to give your bird-loving friends.

INGREDIENTS
Suet
Seeds or dried fruit
¼″ ribbon

EQUIPMENT
Cookie pan
Foil
Cookie cutters

1 Melt the suet, and mix in seeds or dried fruit.

2 Pour onto a foil-lined cookie sheet. Allow to cool completely.

3 With cookie cutters dipped in warm water, cut holiday shapes.

4 Make a hole in the top of each ornament and thread ribbon through so you can hang them.

Suet Swag ❧

Make a swag from strips of cotton rags tied loosely around a cord. Attach suet ornaments to the swag and hang outdoors. You will be providing winter food and nesting materials at the same time.

A Garden Mix

Plant a combination of perennials and annuals to bring droves of birds to your garden. Use a selection from these lists to have flowers — and birds — from spring through fall. For gifts, either mix all the selected seeds together in a cloth bag or bundle individual seed packets together and tie them with a ribbon.

PERENNIAL FLOWER ATTRACTORS

Aubrieta
Bergamot
Columbine
Delphinium
Foxglove
Hollyhock
Lavender
Milkweed
Oregano
Penstemon
Primrose
Stock
Sunflower
Thyme
Trumpet flower

ANNUAL FLOWER ATTRACTORS

Aster
Cornflower
Marigold
Nasturtium

Hummingbird Seed Mix ∾

Hummers like brightly colored flowers, preferably red. Flowers with long throats and sweet nectar are sure to attract these feisty fliers, as well as butterflies. Both birds and butterflies offer hours of riveting, colorful theater.

Fuchsia
Honeysuckle
Impatiens
Nicotiana
Petunia
Trumpet vine

Pinecone Ornaments

Children will love making these bird-feeding ornaments. They'll have fun learning about nature as they contemplate — and supply — the needs of our feathered friends. When melting suet, use a very low flame; it can easily ignite if it gets too hot. Allow to cool slightly before handling.

MATERIALS

Use ¾–1 cup of each per medium to
  large cone:
  Suet
  Birdseed
Pinecones
Florist's wire, 18 gauge
Clean cotton rags, torn into 1″ strips

EQUIPMENT

Cupcake pan with paper liners

1 Melt half the suet and pour into paper-lined cupcake forms, filling cups ¾ of the way.

2 Let suet cool slightly. Press the wide end of a pinecone into each suet compartment. Let cool completely.

3 Remove pinecones from the pan. They should have a base of suet attached. Peel off the paper cups and discard.

4 Wrap florist's wire around the top of each pinecone and form a loop for hanging.

5 Melt a second pan of suet just until soft and dip pinecones into it. You may need to let cool and dip again to get a good coverage. Sprinkle birdseed onto the cooling suet.

6 Tie the cotton rags into a bow at the top of each pinecone.

7 Hang outside for the birds to enjoy.

VARIATIONS:

- Add raisins or dried currants to melted suet before pouring into cupcake tins. You can also press raisins or dried currants into the pinecones before dipping them into melted suet.

- Tear rag strips into 3″ lengths. Fold in half and dip folds into melted suet, then press into pinecones. This will provide nesting materials for home-building birds.

- Cut oranges, grapefruit, or coconuts in half. Scoop out the fruit. Pour melted suet into the empty fruit cups. Use florist's wire to hang these suet holders from tree branches for a colorful wintertime treat.

Thieving Birds ∿

Pine Siskins, who hide their nests in evergreens, are one of many birds these feeders may attract. Found all over the country, they can be aggressive at feeders and are not above stealing seeds from other birds. If your seed mix includes millet, hemp, nutmeats, or sunflower seed, be prepared for droves of these finches.

Birding Groups ∿

National Audubon Society
700 Broadway
New York, NY 10003
212/979-3000
www.audubon.org

American Birding Association
P.O. Box 6599
Colorado Springs, CO 80934
1-800-634-7736
www.americanbirding.org

Canadian Nature Federation
1 Nicholas Street, Suite 606
Ottawa, Ontario K1N 7B7
Canada
613-562-3447
www.web.net/~cnf

Decorated Bird Seed Bag

This is a beautiful way to package the birdseed mixes you make as gifts. Make several and fill with a variety of birdseed. Put them in a basket for a great gift. You'll want to keep one for your own use!

MATERIALS

Stencil Mylar
Cotton canvas or broadcloth, white
  or cream colored, 11″ x 37″
Fabric paint
1 yard twine or cord

EQUIPMENT

Sharp knife or X-acto
Stencil brush
Needle and thread
Sewing machine
Measuring tape
Scissors

Note: Seam allowance is ½ inch.

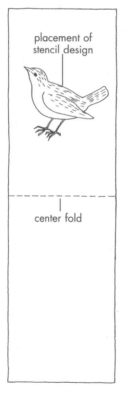

placement of
stencil design

center fold

1 Enlarge the pattern on .page 109. Transfer to the Mylar and cut out the design with a sharp blade. Stencil the design on your cloth using fabric paint and let dry for 24 hours.

2 Fold the cloth in half, right sides together. The design will be on the inside. Pin or baste to hold fabric in place.

3 On one side edge, mark 1½″ from the top edge. Sew the side seams using ½″ allowances, stopping at the marked point on one side. Sew again ⅛″ into seam allowance to add strength. Trim close to stitching.

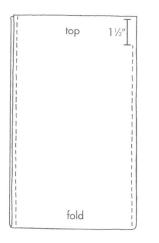

4 Turn the bag right side out. Turn down the top edge of the bag ½″ and press. Turn down again 1″ to form a casing. Sew ⅛″ away from the bottom edge of the casing, and again ¼″.

5 Insert the cord through the casing. Place the two ends of the cord together and tie a knot.

6 Fill with one of the birdseed mixes and give to a friend to enjoy.

Variations

- For an inexpensive "found" mix, recycle bread crumbs, melon, squash, and pumpkin seeds, and muffin and cracker crumbs.

- A true gourmet mix for the birds could include coconut, which chickadees like, a variety of dried fruits, and almost any kind of nuts.

- Tailor your mix to the types of birds (see page 17) your friends want to attract. Name the mix and stitch, stencil, or paint the label on the bag.

Bird-Feeding Wreath

This wreath is so beautiful that you'll want to hang it in your house. Resist this urge, though. Put it outside where you can enjoy the visual feast and the birds can simply feast.

MATERIALS

Straw wreath, 10″–12″ in diameter
18-gauge florist's wire, cut into
   12″ lengths
2 oranges
3 pinecones
1 cup peanut butter or suet
1 cup birdseed
2 apples
2 yards string or strong thread
1 pound fresh cranberries
6 cups air-popped popcorn
Scraps of clean cotton fabric,
   approximately ⅛ yard

1 Bend 12″ of florist's wire to form a loop for hanging the wreath. Attach to the back of the wreath.

back

2 Cut the oranges in half. Cut a 12″ length of wire and fold it in half. Push both ends of the wire through the orange and then secure them to the wreath.

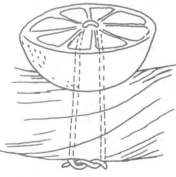

3 Twist a piece of wire around the top of a pinecone, leaving tails long enough to attach the cone to the wreath. Smear liberally with peanut butter or slightly warmed suet. Roll the pinecones in the birdseed and attach to the wreath, alternating with the oranges.

4 Cut the apples in half and treat the same way as you did the oranges. Place them in the spaces between the pinecones and oranges.

5 String 1 yard each of cranberries and popcorn onto the thread or string. Wrap the strings of berries and popcorn around the wreath.

6 Tear the cotton scraps into 2" wide strips. Lay several together and tie a piece around the middle to form a bow. Using a length of wire, attach it to wreath at the lower right side. You can also use bits of the cotton strips, folded in half and wired to the wreath, to fill in any gaps between the fruit and pinecones.

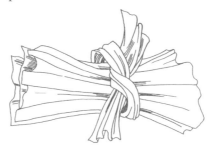

7 Hang on a tree trunk or barn door. Birds will flock to it.

Basket of Foliage

Place this basket under a window to get a good view of the birds as they eat the offerings and just to appreciate the beauty of the arrangement.

MATERIALS

Basket
Waterproof container
Florist's foam
Branches from any of the following plants, cut when fruiting or, for the sunflower, when the seeds have matured:

Black cherry	Blueberry
Dogwood	Eastern white pine
Elderberry	Grape
Hawthorn	Holly
Honeysuckle	Juniper
Mountain ash	Maple
Mulberry	Oak
Red cedar	Sumac
Sunflower	Virginia creeper

Arrange the branches in the basket and place near the feeding area. This is an especially nice gift if your bird-loving friend does not have a landscape that is naturally full of plants that birds like.

Seed Scoop

This handy tool will be even more prized because you made it. Simple techniques make this easy, and readily available; recycled tin cans make it an inexpensive gift.

MATERIALS

1 piece of lumber, 1″ x 6″
1 sheet of tin, 11″ x 9″
One 6″ length of ¾″ dowel
Wood glue
One 1″ wooden ball
4 small wood screws
1 wood screw, 1½″ long

EQUIPMENT

Jigsaw or keyhole saw
Drill and ¾″ drill bit
Tin snips or strong shears
Screwdriver
File or emery cloth
Sandpaper, coarse, medium,
  and fine grit

1 Cut the circle for the back of the scoop out of the 1″ lumber. Drill a ¾″ hole in the center.

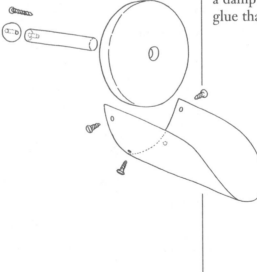

2 Run a thin bead of glue on the inside of the hole. Insert the dowel into the hole until it is flush with the opposite side. Use a damp rag to wipe away any glue that squeezes out.

3 Drill a small hole at the other end of the dowel, and drill a small hole through the wooden ball. Use a long screw to attach the ball to the end of the dowel. With wood glue, secure the ball tightly to the dowel. Let dry for several hours. Sand and finish the wooden pieces before attaching to the metal.

4 Cut out the tin scoop using tin snips or a strong pair of shears. (See pages 102–103 for techniques for preparing a tin sheet.) Smooth edges with a file and emery cloth. Drill four small holes along the straight edge of the scoop piece. (You will attach the scoop to the handle portion by screwing through these holes.)

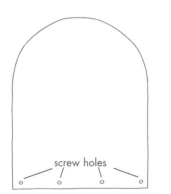

5 Form the scoop by bending the tin around another tin can, 6″ in diameter. Run a bead of wood glue between the screw holes and attach the scoop to the edge of the round wooden backing with the four small screws. Allow the glue to dry.

VARIATION

Cover the dowel handle and wooden ball with polymer clay for a customized grip. Get wild — use bright-colored canes and rolled swirls. Both the metal and wood covered with the clay can be baked in your oven on low, as long as you have not used any finishing medium on the wooden parts such as varnish, paint, or shellac.

(See pages 102–103 for techniques for preparing a tin sheet.)

Ways to Make Feeders Squirrelproof ∾

Squirrels are wily creatures who will probably figure out ways to defeat your best efforts. But try hanging feeders from a pole using wires instead of hanging them from trees. Invert a tin pie pan above a wire-hung feeder; it makes a good baffle.

Seed Bin

Everyone who feeds birds needs a safe place to store seed mix. Squirrels and mice often make short work of seed kept in bags in the garage. This wooden bin is an attractive solution that will please anyone on your gift list.

MATERIALS

Six 12″ squares of ¾″ lumber
2 pieces of lumber 10½″ square
1 drawer pull or knob
20 wood screws, 1¼″ long
Wood glue
1 small tube of silicone caulk

EQUIPMENT

Table or circular saw
Drill and ⅛″ bits
Screwdriver

CREATING THE BOX

1 Cut the lumber to the needed sizes. Miter corners of the four side pieces to 45 degrees.

2 Predrill the holes for screws on the corners. Form into a cube using screws and glue. The corners will be 90 degrees when finished.

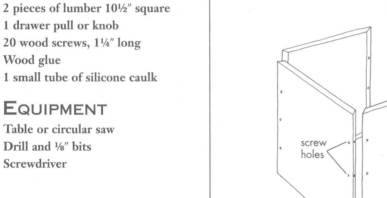

screw
holes

12″

12″

mitered corner

3 Cut the bottom piece of lumber to fit inside the cube. Predrill along the lower edge of the cube's inside pieces so that you can secure the bottom in place with screws. Insert the bottom so that it is flush with the lower edge of the cube. Secure with four screws and glue. Run a bead of silicone along the inside corners to help make the bin waterproof.

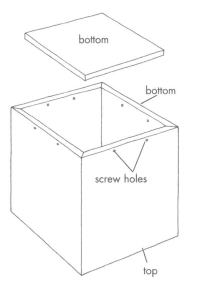

bottom

bottom

screw holes

top

CREATING THE TOP

4 Cut a piece of lumber to fit inside the cube at the top, approximately 10½″ square. Center this on another piece of lumber cut equal to the size of the outside of the cube. Center the smaller piece on the underside of the larger piece and glue. Secure with four screws.

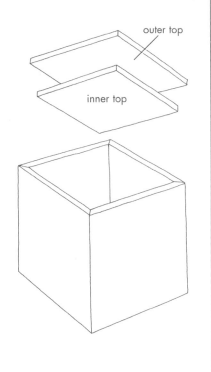

outer top

inner top

5 Finish as desired! You can paint or stain the bins, and for fun accents, use one of the designs from other projects in this book and paint or stencil.

6 Drill a hole in the top for the drawer pull. Attach the drawer pull with a screw.

VARIATION
Line the inside of the seed bin with tin to deter rodents even more effectively.

Muffins

Even birds like special treats. Bake these goodies and give them to your favorite feathered friends. Just make sure to avoid mixing them with your own breakfast muffins!

INGREDIENTS

2 cups cornmeal
½ teaspoon soda
¼ teaspoon salt
1 cup buttermilk
1 cup meat or fat scraps
Dash of clean sand

1 Mix all ingredients and pour the mixture into greased or papered muffin cups.

2 Bake at 425°F for 20 minutes. Cool, peel off the paper linings, and place the muffins outside on platform feeders.

VARIATION:

You can add nut meats, fruit, or seeds to make this a treat that no bird will be able to resist.

Birdscaping Plants ～

You can use your landscaping to attract birds year-round. Birds need plants that offer places to hide, to nest, to shelter, to eat and drink. Provide the right habitat and you'll have great success.

Some plants that birds find irresistible are shrub roses, firs, junipers, mulberries, blackberries, oaks, and sumacs.

Birds love to nest in hawthorns, hollies, and hackberries. These prickly plants help deter predators.

CHAPTER 3

Gifts for the Garden

*M*id pleasures and palaces though we may roam,
Be it ever so humble, there's no place like home;
A charm from the skies seems to hallow us there,
Which sought through the world is ne'er met with elsewhere.

An exile from home splendour dazzles in vain,
Oh give me my lowly thatched cottage again;
The birds singing gayly, that came at my call,
Give me them, and that peace of mind dearer than all.
Home, Sweet Home.
— J. Howard Payne. 1792–1852,
from the opera of *Clari, the Maid of Milan*

If you offer birds food, shelter, and water they will soon make a home in your garden. Not only will their beauty and song delight you, but they will provide ecological bug control. The easy projects in this chapter are sure to encourage many birds to set up housekeeping in your yard.

Hanging Ceramic Birdbath

Birds love to bathe, and you'll love watching their antics. Give them a safe and colorful place to get clean by making this hanging bath. Keep it full of clean fresh water and the birds will flock to it.

MATERIALS

¾" plywood disk, 12" in diameter
1 rimmed ceramic flowerpot saucer,
   8" in diameter
Acrylic paint
Marine-grade varnish (optional)
4 screw eyes with ¾" shanks
Sturdy hook
4 yards wire, chain, or stout cord
2" metal ring

EQUIPMENT

Jigsaw or scroll saw
Paintbrush
Drill and bits, ⅛"

1 Set the saucer in the center of the plywood. Trace a line around the bottom edge of the saucer. Following your line, cut out the center of the circle to create a place to nestle the saucer. Paint the plywood with several coats of acrylic paint. Consider using a layer of marine-grade varnish as the top coat: Bathing birds will keep soaking the wood, and this will help prevent decay.

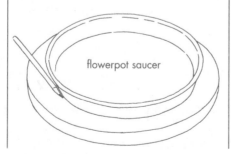

flowerpot saucer

2 Space the screw eyes equally around the plywood, about 1" from the outer edge. Dab a small amount of glue on the thread before you attach the screw eyes. This will keep them secured to the wood.

3 Cut the cord or wire into two equal lengths. Tie one end of a piece of cord to a screw eye. Tie one end of the second piece of cord to an adjacent screw eye. Push the untied ends of the cords through the metal ring and tie them to the screw eyes on the opposite edge of the circle.

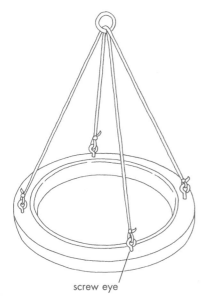

screw eye

4 Put the saucer into the hole in the painted plywood.

5 Secure a sturdy metal screw hook into a tree limb, and hang the birdbath from it, slipping the metal ring onto the hook. (Position the birdbath where it's easy to reach for cleaning and refilling.) Fill it with water and place a few pebbles in the saucer to give the birds a place to stand.

Why Do Birds Take Baths? ∾

Birds take baths, in water or in dust, and they are constantly preening: rearranging ruffled feathers with their bills or beaks, re-zipping separated barbules, preparing the feathers for flight. Birds don't preen to make themselves look pretty; preening is an essential form of equipment maintenance. Don't think of a movie star primping in front of a mirror: Think of a flight mechanic readying a machine for take-off.

Hypertufa Birdbath

Hypertufa is a mixture of sand, cement, peat moss, and water that can be poured into a mold and allowed to harden until it forms a lightweight faux stone. There is something about this project that brings out the child in everyone who tries it, perhaps because it's so much fun getting in there and playing with the "mud." Once you get going, who knows what you'll make?

MATERIALS

1–2 gallons of clean masonry sand
Portland cement
Milled peat moss
Water

EQUIPMENT

Bucket
Round, flat-bottomed plastic container 1′–2′ in diameter, 6″–8″ deep

1 Form a mound in the middle of the plastic container using clean sand. Smooth and firm it. You can be creative by embedding leaves, twigs, feathers, and small pebbles in the surface of the sand.

2 Make the hypertufa in the bucket, using equal parts concrete, sand, and peat moss. Add water until the mixture is the consistency of cookie dough. Pour into the plastic container. Gently knock against the sides of the container to get good contact between the hypertufa and the sand. Allow the hypertufa to dry for 24 to 48 hours.

3 Remove the birdbath from the plastic container. Allow the birdbath to cure for 4 to 6 weeks. After this first curing period, place the birdbath outside and rinse it frequently to remove chemicals and neutralize cement. It will be safe to use in about 3 more weeks.

4 You can distress the birdbath to add texture and the illusion of age by hacking, whacking, and chiseling with various tools, such as chisels and hatchets.

5 This birdbath is too heavy to hang. Instead, place it on a tree stump, a flat-topped rock, or a stone wall.

Make a Concrete Birdbath to Cover with Mosaic ∾

Use a concrete mix to make a birdbath following the directions for the hypertufa bath then cover the outside with a pebble mosaic. You can set the pebbles using either a tile mastic or a base of wet mortar. For a special look, combine river pebbles with lapidary-cut stones, available at craft stores. Fill in spaces between pebbles with mortar. When finished, cover with a damp cloth to let the mortar dry slowly. To keep the cloth damp you can either mist it occasionally or cover it with a plastic sheet.

Keeping Predators at Bay ∾

It can sharply decrease your enjoyment of birdwatching to see the neighborhood cat hanging around your feeder or birdbath. Put feeders on poles with a metal sleeve to keep cats from climbing the pole. You can also help the birds by belling your cat. But raccoons, opossums, and other birds, too, eat eggs, nestlings, and even adult birds.

When building nesting boxes, reinforce the opening with a square piece of wood, slightly larger than the opening. Screw or glue this piece to the front of the nesting box and drill the opening through both thicknesses. Don't put perches on the nesting boxes; they just give predator birds a place to sit.

Wren Nesting Box

Wrens are among the easiest of birds to attract to nesting boxes. The male prepares the nest in hopes of attracting a mate; often he'll maintain more than one nest, to give a prospective mate a selection and to broaden the territory that appears to be taken. So make several for these feathered scalawags.

MATERIALS

Redwood or cedar, ¾″ stock
  For the roof:
    A: 9″ x 7″
    B: 9″ x 6¼″
  For the sides:
    C: 5″ x 5″
    D: 5″ x 4¼″
  For the front:
    E: 5″ x 5″
  For the back:
    F: 5″ x 5″
2 eye bolts, 1½″ x ³⁄₁₆″ shank,
  with washers and nuts
Twenty 1″ brass screws
1 tube of silicone glue

EQUIPMENT

Table or circular saw
Drill and drill bits, ⅛″, ¼″, ⅞″–1⅛″
  (for opening)
Screwdriver

1 Measure and cut out two roof pieces (A and B). Predrill the two nail holes along the crest line end of the 9″ x 6¼″ roof piece. Apply the glue to the end of the 9″ x 7″ board. Nail to the predrilled 9″ x 6¼″ roof piece at a 90-degree angle. Wipe away any excess glue with a damp cloth.

2 Measure and cut the side pieces. Drill ¼″ holes 1″ apart and 1″ from the edge along the top and bottom. (This is to provide drainage and ventilation in the birdhouse.)

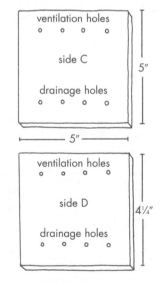

side C — 5″ — 5″
ventilation holes
drainage holes

side D — 4¼″
ventilation holes
drainage holes

3 Predrill the holes for the screws on the 5″ x 5″ side piece. Connect the sides at a 90-degree angle. If you have used nails to construct the rest of the wren house, use screws for this joint, and to connect the 5″ x 5″ side piece to the roof. This allows you to open the nesting box for annual cleaning. With screws, connect the sides to the roof.

4 Drill the roof down through the crest line and put the eye bolts through the holes. Secure with washers and nuts. Run a bead of silicone glue on the inside of the eave and to seal around the eye bolts. This will keep the wrens safe and dry.

5 Cut the front and back pieces. Measure and cut the opening in the front. It should be 1″–1½″ from the top and ⅞″–1⅛″ in diameter. Predrill holes along the lower edges of the front and back. Use screws to attach to the ends of the side pieces.

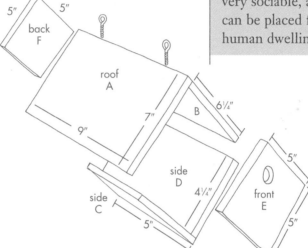

Gift Idea ∾

When you give this gift, attach a small card letting the recipient know that the nesting box should be placed facing south and 5 to 10 feet above the ground. Wrens are very sociable, and their boxes can be placed fairly close to human dwellings.

Basic Nesting Box

Build a nesting box to welcome a variety of birds to your yard and garden. Use the dimensions here or adapt to attract specific birds, following the suggestions in the chart on page 42.

MATERIALS

Lumber, ¾″
  Back: 5″ x 12″
  Front: 5″ x 9″
  Roof: one 6″ x 8″ and one 6″ x 7¼″
  Sides: two 4¼″ x 6¼″
  Bottom: 4¼″ x 5″
Sandpaper
Wood glue or silicone
Screws

EQUIPMENT

Table or circular saw
Jigsaw or scroll saw
Drill and drill bits, ⅛″ and ⅞″–1⅛″
  (for opening)
Screwdriver

1 Cut lumber into the seven pieces you'll need. Lightly sand edges to remove burrs.

2 Predrill three screw holes along one short side of the larger roof piece. Run a bead of glue or silicone along the end of the smaller roof piece. Lap the larger piece over the other at a 90-degree angle. Secure with three screws.

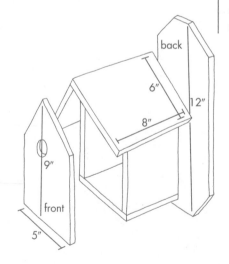

3 Taper one end (the top) of each side piece to make a 45° angle. Drill ventilation holes 1″ below the top of the sides. Make drainage holes in the bottom piece.

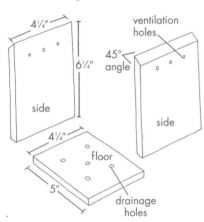

4 Predrill the screw holes in the floor. *Note:* Don't glue or silicone this section because you'll want to be able to remove the bottom for annual cleaning.

5 Make the entrance hole in the front piece. It should be between ⅞″ and 1⅛″. Predrill the screw holes and attach the front. You can use a bead of glue along the sides, but remember, not the bottom.

6 Predrill the screw holes on the back and attach to the rest of the birdhouse.

7 Finish as desired. You may paint or stencil your nesting box.

Bluebirds ❧

Bluebirds are especially helpful to humankind. Three-quarters of their diet consists of crop-destroying insects such as grasshoppers, caterpillars, beetles, and corn borers. They sometimes breed twice in one summer. Bluebirds like fence rows. Place bluebird houses along them 3–5 feet above the ground, spacing them about 100 yards apart.

Robin Shelf

Robins and phoebes both prefer roofed but open-fronted shelves for nesting. This rustic nesting shelf will invite both of these marvelous birds to settle in your neighborhood. You will soon have your own feathered bug-fighting brigade. As robins need mud for nesting material, to attract robins to your shelf place a shallow pan nearby and fill it with soil which is high in clay content. Keep it wet and sticky.

1 Measure and cut wood to the dimensions indicated in the materials list.

2 Predrill screw holes as shown in each piece. Predrill the drainage holes.

MATERIALS

Lumber — cedar shakes, firewood slabs, pressure treated
  Back: 7½″ x 12″
  Top: 7½″ x 6″
  Bottom: 7½″ x 6″
  Front: 7½″ x 2″
  Sides: two 6″ x 8″
Twenty-five 1½″ screws, two 2″ screws
1 tube of silicone glue

EQUIPMENT

Table or circular saw
Drill and drill bits
Screwdriver

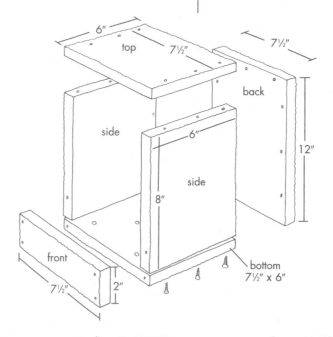

3 Attach the top to the sides with a bead of glue and screws. You can be liberal in your use of glue; since this box is virtually open in front, it's exposed to plenty of weather.

4 Attach the bottom piece to the sides by applying a bead of glue and then securing it in place with screws.

5 Finish the shelf by attaching the front and back sections to your structure with glue and screws.

6 Hang the nesting shelf by drilling through the back at top and bottom and attaching to a tree, building, or fence post with 2″ screws. It's preferable to hang the shelf 6 to 10 feet off the ground in a sheltered location.

Feeding Tips ∿

When you think about where to place a bird feeder, consider whether you want to be able to watch the activity from your house. Make sure it's easy to reach year-round; when it becomes a popular hangout for the birds, you'll be filling it often — more often if squirrels come by for a meal. Birds are messy; will the location become unsightly? Most birds like to have some shrubbery within a few yards of the feeder. This gives them a safe place to sit while awaiting their turn.

Spruce Up Your Birdhouses ∿

- ∿ Cover them with split twigs for a rustic look.
- ∿ Use cedar shingles to cover the roof.
- ∿ Paint with dark, muted colors, like dark green, brown, and dark blue.

Birdhouse Dimension Chart ～

The entrance hole to a nesting box should be on the front and near the top. Each species is particular about dimensions for the opening. This chart shows good housing and entrance dimensions for some of the most common birds.

Species	Floor Plan	Depth (in inches)	Entrance above Floor (in inches)	Diameter of Entrance (in inches)	Height above Ground (in feet)
Wren	4x4	6–8	1–6	1	6–10
Chickadee	4x4	8–10	6–8	1⅛	6–15
Nuthatch	4x4	8–10	6–8	1¼	12–20
Titmouse	4x4	8–10	6–8	1¼	6–15
Bluebird	5x8	6	1½		10–15
Robin	6x8	8	one side open		6–15
Barn swallow	6x6	6	one side open		8–12
Song sparrow	6x6	6	all sides open		1–3
Phoebe	6x6	6	one side open		8–12
Purple martin	6x6	6	one side open		15–20

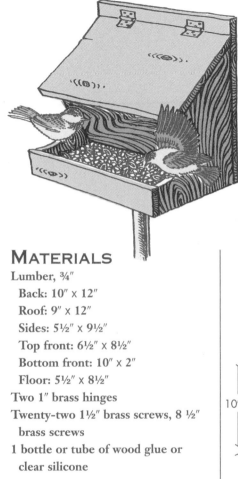

Hopper Feeder

This is one of the most popular kinds of feeders. It is constructed to refill the tray as the birds eat the seed. It can be suspended from a tree or put on a pole. This is a great opportunity to find out who is more devious, you or the squirrel.

MATERIALS

Lumber, ¾"
  Back: 10" x 12"
  Roof: 9" x 12"
  Sides: 5½" x 9½"
  Top front: 6½" x 8½"
  Bottom front: 10" x 2"
  Floor: 5½" x 8½"
Two 1" brass hinges
Twenty-two 1½" brass screws, 8 ½"
  brass screws
1 bottle or tube of wood glue or
  clear silicone

EQUIPMENT

Table or circular saw
Jigsaw or scroll saw
Drill and ⅛" drill bit
Screwdriver

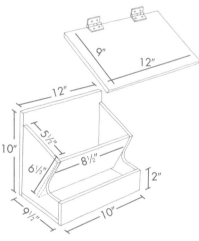

1 Cut the sides. Assemble the top front by attaching it flush to the front edge of the sides and flush to the top edge. Attach the bottom front to the lower lip of the sides.

2 Drill small drainage holes in the bottom piece. Slide the bottom into the space between the sides and bottom front and attach with glue and screws.

3 Attach to the back, flush to the bottom edge of the back piece.

4 Place the hinges on the top back edge of the roof piece, 2" from the sides. Fasten with glue and screws. Attach to the back board. Allow glue to dry.

5 Fill with seed and make way for the visitors.

Tray and Suet Feeder

This feeder, which holds both seeds and suet, will attract a variety of birds. You can use commercial suet holders or make your own out of ½" hardware cloth. Try your hand at making your own suet from one of the recipes in this book.

MATERIALS

Lumber, ¾"
  Two uprights: 6" x 8" (refer to the diagram)
  Bottom: 8½" x 10½"
  2 sides: 2" x 12"
  2 ends: 2" x 8½"
2 commercial suet boxes
2 screw eyes big enough to support the feeder
4 cup hooks
½" dowel, 8" long
Twenty-four 1½" brass screws
1 tube of silicone glue
14 gauge wire for hanging

EQUIPMENT

Table or circular saw
Jigsaw or scroll saw
Drill and drill bits, ⅛" and ½"
Screwdriver

1 Referring to the exploded drawings, cut the uprights and drill the hole for the dowel. Run a small bead of glue inside the hole for the dowel. Connect the uprights with the dowel. The ends of the dowel should be flush with the outside of the uprights. The bottoms of the uprights should line up in order to lie flat against the tray. Use a damp cloth to wipe away any excess glue. Set aside to dry.

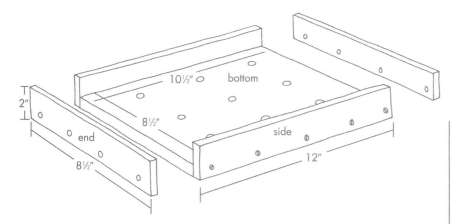

2 In the bottom piece, drill ³⁄₁₆″ drainage holes about 1″–2″ apart. Assemble the seed tray by attaching the sides and then the ends with glue and screws. The bottom edges of the sides and ends should be flush with the bottom of the tray.

3 Attach the uprights to the bottom by predrilling up through the bottom. Use screws and glue to connect. Wipe away any excess glue with a damp rag. Place two cup hooks on the outside of each upright, 5″ up from the bottom and 2″–3″ apart. Hang the suet holders on the cup hooks.

4 Put the screw eyes into the uprights. Hang the feeder from a branch or taut laundry line.

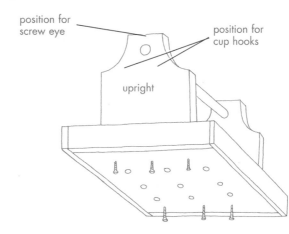

position for screw eye

position for cup hooks

upright

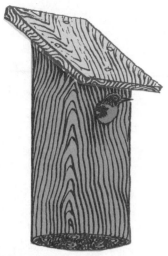

Hollowed Log House

If you have a 16"–20" section of cedar post and a cedar shingle, you have the makings of a perfect birdhouse.

MATERIALS
16"–20" piece of cedar post
Cedar shingle

EQUIPMENT
Drill, with ⅞"–1" bit
Saw

1 Using a ⅞"–1" bit on a drill, bore out the center of the cedar post (from the top, vertically) until you have a cavity 4"–6" in diameter. Leave a floor 2"–3" thick.

2 Make the opening 2" wide to attract the red-headed woodpecker, or 3" for the screech owl and kestrels.

3 Saw off the top at an angle. Screw the shingle on to create a roof.

4 Add drainage holes in the floor and ventilation holes in the sides near the roof.

5 Place your hollowed log house on top of an old tree stump or hang it on a tree 10 to 30 feet off the ground.

To hang: remove the roof and, going through the opening, drill a hole through the back with a long-shanked drill bit. Attach with long screws and replace the roof.

Where to Place Birdhouses ∾

Remember that you will want to be able to access the birdhouse for periodic cleaning. Keep the number of birdhouses for a single species to a minimum. Birds are territorial little creatures and don't appreciate urban sprawl of the avian kind. Don't put birdhouses near bird feeders; close proximity encourages territorial battles, and feathers will fly. In general, you will be more successful if your birdhouses are oriented with their entrances facing south.

CHAPTER 4

Gifts for the Home

*A*t the close of the day when the hamlet is still,

And mortals the sweets of forgetfulness prove,

When naught but the torrent is heard on the hill,

And naught but the nightingale's song in the grove.

— James Beattie (1735–1803), *The Hermit*

Using birds and birdhouses as motifs adds a whimsical touch to any decor. You will find a variety of gift projects to bring out the folk artist in you. Have fun and be creative!

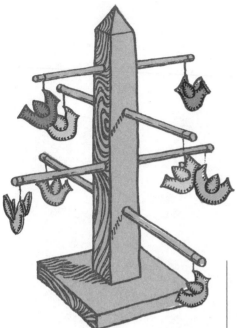

Bird Tree

This bird tree can be adapted to various occasions by changing the colors and fabrics. The folksy design fits charmingly into almost any decor. Use a found branch for a natural look.

MATERIALS

One 20″ length of 2″x2″ lumber or
  purchased tree form
½″ dowel, 52″ long
One 6″ square of 1″ lumber (bottom)
1½″ screw
Sandpaper
Scraps of wool, felt, and trimmings,
  to make birds
White glue
Embroidery floss or perle cotton
Fusible web
Paint, as desired

EQUIPMENT

Saw
Drill and ½″ drill bit

TREE

1 *If you are making your tree:* Angle the top of the 2″ x 2″ lumber by making a series of 45-degree cuts on each side of one end. This will give you a pyramid shape for the top. Sand to smooth the wood.

2 Cut the ½″ dowel into 10″, 12″, 14″, and 16″ pieces.

3 Drill ½″ holes 4″ apart into the 2″ x 2″, alternating sides.

4 Slide dowels through holes and center each in the post.

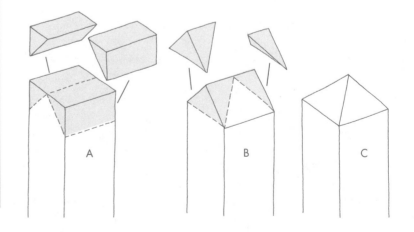

5 Drill a small hole in the center of the 6″ x 6″ bottom. Predrill a hole in the bottom of the post. Cover the bottom edge with glue. With a screw, attach to the post. Wipe away any extra glue with a damp cloth.

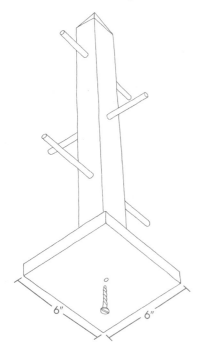

6 *Finish as desired:* You can paint with acrylics, spray paint with a metallic paint, or give it a faux finish.

BIRDS

7 Transfer the pattern (see page 109) to the felt or wool. Cut two pieces of felt or wool slightly larger than the pattern. Attach together using a fusible web and cut into the bird shape.

8 Using fabric for the wings, fuse two pieces together as in step 7. Cut out wings and glue or sew to the body. Cut out the beak from a single layer of fabric and glue or sew to the bird.

9 Using a piece of floss or perle cotton, blanket-stitch around the outside edge of the bird, around wings, and around other raw edges.

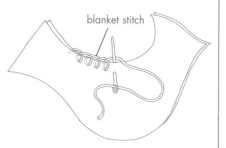

blanket stitch

10 Use an 8″ length of floss or perle cotton to hang the bird. Adjust the length as needed to fit on the tree.

11 Repeat steps 7–10 to make birds for each branch. The birds should swing freely.

A Natural Tree

∾ Find a suitable tree branch and mount it in a small can using plaster of Paris. Set the can in a ginger jar. Hang origami cranes (see pages 105–107 for techniques) on fish line. Make the cranes in a variety of sizes and colors.

∾ Use this tree as a table decoration at Easter. Hang colored, blown eggs and your birds from the branches. It will be a gay celebration of the return of spring.

Canvas Floorcloth

This painted canvas floorcloth is surprisingly durable, but it's beautiful enough to hang on the wall. It can take the traffic any teenager can give and still clean up to look good for company.

MATERIALS

20″ x 26″ cotton canvas
1 jar of gesso
Sponge brush
Acrylic paints
Clear acrylic spray finish

1 Turn under the edges of the canvas ½″ and stitch. Turn under again and stitch to give a finished edge.

2 Using the sponge brush, paint on the gesso in three light coats, letting it dry and sanding lightly between applications. Alternate directions of your brush strokes with each coat.

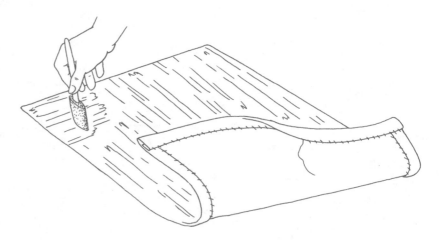

3 Enlarge and cut out patterns on page 109. Trace birds in a design of your choice on canvas. Add whatever background decoration you wish, using drawing of finished floorcloth for inspiration.

4 Paint your design, creating red birds with yellow and orange beaks, black or brown feet, and black "Welcome" letters on a yellow or red background, all bordered in black; or use a color scheme that complements your own home.
You can customize the design any way you like. Get wild and have fun!

5 Apply three light coats of the spray finish. Allow to dry thoroughly between applications.

VARIATIONS
Painted canvas cloths do more than just lie on your floor. The rugged finish on the final product stands up to much rough usage. Consider these ideas and then try out some of your own inventions:

- Use canvas and this painting technique to create a beach bag with brightly colored parrots on it.

- Stencil a bird on a canvas wallet.

- Sew a custom tablecloth for your picnic table, and paint bird tracks across it.

Grouse

Nature Prints

Use the beauty of feathers to decorate stationery, note cards, and bookmarks. The best time to gather feathers is during molting season (see page 53).

MATERIALS

Variety of small feathers
Stamp pad and ink
Assortment of papers

EQUIPMENT

Brayer (optional)
Tweezers

1 After you've decided whether you'll decorate a bookmark, stationery, or note cards, and you've selected the paper for it, plan where you want to set the feather print on the paper.

2 Place the feather on the ink pad and cover it with a piece of scrap paper. Gently press the feather into the ink with your fingers or a brayer (a small roller used in printmaking) to ensure good contact with ink.

3 With tweezers, remove the feather from the ink pad. Place the inked feather on good paper and cover it with a clean piece of scrap paper. Gently press or use a brayer to leave an ink print of the feather on your paper.

4 Carefully remove the feather and allow the ink to dry.

Molting Seasons ∽

Canada goose	summer
Chimney swift	late summer/ before migration
Crow	summer
Blue jay	July and August
Robin	July and August
Black-capped chickadee	July and August
House sparrow	late summer
Common grackle	August and September

More Nature Prints ∽

- ∽ With so many applications for this craft, you needn't limit yourself to printing only on paper or fabric. All you have to do is look around you to find more ways to use the feather printing technique for a variety of projects.
- ∽ Decorate terra cotta pots with feather prints.
- ∽ Sponge paint a texture on bandboxes and stamp a line of feathers around the sides.
- ∽ Make a book jacket out of heavy brown paper and place a gold feather on the front. You can laminate the jacket with clear plastic to make it more durable.

Switch Plate

Give any room a whimsical touch with one of these delightful light switch plates. Children especially will love to have these in their rooms. Get your inspiration from pictures of large, colorful birds, and be sure to use bright colors when you carry out your design.

MATERIALS

Metal switch plate
Polymer clay for clay switch plate
Sheet metal for tin switch plate
Color photocopies of pictures of birds, wrapping paper or napkins for technique 3
Decoupage medium for technique 3

Polymer Clay Switch Plate

1 Condition clay (see pages 104–105 for techniques). Roll out a piece to about ⅛″ thick, and slightly larger than the switch plate. Place over the switch plate and press lightly to get good contact between the metal and clay. With a sharp knife, transfer the holes and openings to the clay, and trim the edges.

2 Roll out 1″ balls of polymer clay to ¼″ thickness. Using a sharp knife, cut out simple bird shapes. As a guide, use any of the patterns from this book, or make your own. Place one in the upper-right-hand corner of

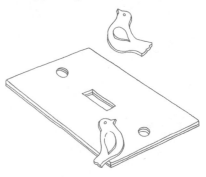

the plate so that the bird extends slightly past the edge of the plate. The second bird goes in the lower-left-hand corner of the plate.

3 Bake according to manufacturer's instructions and finish as desired.

VARIATION

To make a birdhouse switch plate, make a roof out of two colors of brown polymer clay rolled into a cane. Cut the roll into slices and press them onto a flat base layer to give a log cabin look.

Tin Switch Plate

MATERIALS

Tin can
Model enamels

EQUIPMENT

Emery cloth or fine file
Nail driver
Hammer
Tin snips or heavy shears
Epoxy or solder and soldering gun

1 Cut a tin can apart and flatten it. Cut out a simple bird with tin snips or heavy shears.

2 Smooth the edges of the bird with emery paper or a fine file. With a nail punch, score lines to outline the wings, beak, and eyes. You can also paint the birds with bright model enamels.

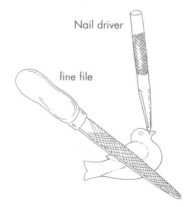

Nail driver

fine file

3 Using an epoxy glue, glue the bird to the switch plate.

Decoupage Switch Plate

1 Cut out bird designs from paper. Using an old paint brush or a small sponge brush, cover the switch plate with the decoupage medium. Press the paper into the medium. Make sure to smooth the paper and remove all wrinkles and air bubbles.

2 With a sharp blade, cut the decoupage paper to expose holes in the switch plate. Tuck the paper behind the light switch to completely cover the switch plate.

3 Apply another coat of decoupage medium over both the paper and any exposed metal. Allow to dry.

Refrigerator Magnet

No bird-lover's refrigerator magnet collection would be complete without one of these handmade beauties.

MATERIALS

Polymer clay
Refrigerator magnet
Silicone glue

1 Condition clay (see pages 104–105 for technique) and roll a small ball in the palm of your hand. Using a flat-sided bottle or rolling pin, flatten to ¼″. Enlarge the pattern below and use to cut out a bird with a sharp knife. Smooth the edges.

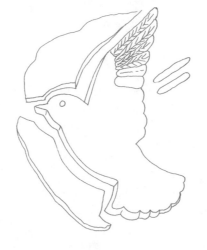

2 Roll small amounts of clay between your fingers into a cigar shape. Flatten slightly. Use a needle or pin to make hatch marks on the flattened clay, to create feathers. Place these feathers on the wings and tail.

3 Bake according to manufacturer's directions.

4 When cool, finish as desired. Using silicone glue, attach the magnet to the back of the bird.

VARIATIONS

Make the birdhouse or nest magnets, following the design shown above.

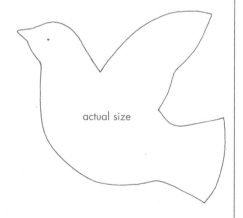

Votive Candleholder

This easy votive candleholder is sure to be a hit at Christmastime. It can be adapted for other holidays by painting after the design has been made. Place several together and surround with greenery for an elegant centerpiece.

MATERIALS

8-ounce tin can
Votive candle
Floral clay
Holly
Glue

actual size

EQUIPMENT

Freezer
Nail punch
Hammer

1 Trace the pattern and cut out. If you have a larger can, enlarge your patttern by photo-copying, or applying a grid (see page 107).

2 Use a washable marker to trace the pattern outline on the side of the can.

3 Fill the can with water and freeze. (The ice supports the can while you punch your design.)

4 Using the nail punch, make the holes for the design. Allow water to melt.

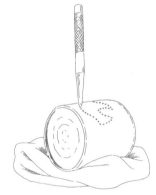

5 Press a small wad of floral clay in the candleholder and firmly push a votive candle into it.

6 Decorate with a few sprigs of holly.

Feather Wreath

Experiment with the feathers you find in sporting goods stores that specialize in supplies for fly fishermen. Use the especially lovely ones to make flowers.

MATERIALS

10″ straw or grapevine wreath
Two 1″ Styrofoam balls
Assorted feathers
3 small strawflowers
Raffia
6 pheasant tail feathers or other
   long feathers
Florist's wire, 18 gauge
White glue

MAKING FEATHER FLOWERS

1 Use a sharp knife to cut the Styrofoam balls in half.

2 Place a small amount of glue on a scrap of paper.

3 Bend three 8″ lengths of wire in half. Push each wire through a Styrofoam half so that

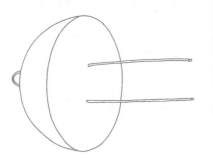

the tails come out the flat side (the back) of the flower.

4 Start at the edge of the back of the flower form, using the largest of your feathers. Touch the quill tip to the glue and push it into the foam. Use a large needle or knitting needle to make a hole if the feather quill is too soft. Work inward

around the Styrofoam ball, using smaller feathers as you get closer to the center.

5 Cut the stem off a strawflower. Glue the strawflower to the center, covering the Styrofoam.

MAKING THE WREATH

6 Bunch three of the tail feathers together and tie the bottom ends with wire. Do the same with the other three tail feathers and place them end to end with the other bunch. The tips should face out. Connect them with wire. Attach the feathers to the lower right of the wreath with a bit of wire.

7 Place the feather flowers over the tail feathers covering the wire. Attach to the wreath with the wire tails on the back of the flowers.

8 Make several small bows with raffia and use to fill in any holes between the flowers.

9 Make a wire loop at the top of the wreath and attach to the back for hanging.

Lovely, but Legal? ❧

Several projects, including this wreath, call for the use of feathers. But many bird lovers know that, in the past, birds were killed by the thousands for their feathers. Because of this, many friends of the birds consider it immoral to use and possess many kinds of feathers.

What most people don't know is that it is illegal to possess many types of feathers. Private citizens can usually own feathers only from birds that were legally killed. Duck, chicken, and pheasant feathers are all safe, for example, if obtained from a reputable source. Owl, eagle, or other protected species' feathers, on the other hand, are not.

Check with local authorities if you are unsure, and always purchase feathers for projects from reputable dealers (such as suppliers of fly-fishing and fly-tying gear).

And for the sake of the feathered citizens of the world, stay away from, or better yet, report, anyone you suspect of having and selling feathers obtained illegally.

Mosaic Trivet

This bright trivet will enliven any bird lover's kitchen. See
pages 101–102 for more information about mosaics.

MATERIALS

12″ square, unfinished, wood picture
   frame (without glass)
¼″ plywood, cut to fit inside the
   frame
Wood glue
Small brads
Ceramic tiles in bright colors or old
   pottery plates
Tile mastic
Masking tape
Grout

EQUIPMENT

Saw
Hammer

1 Use a sturdy base for the mosaic. Glue the plywood securely to the inside of the frame. Use small brads if necessary to make sure that there is no wiggle between the frame and plywood. Cover the frame with masking tape to protect it from mastic and grout.

2 Break the ceramic tiles or pottery by placing them in a double-layered paper bag and hitting with a hammer. Pieces should be at least ½″ by 1″.

3 Use the pattern on page 109 or create your own design.

4 With a pencil, transfer the design to the plywood. Apply mastic to the inside of the design.

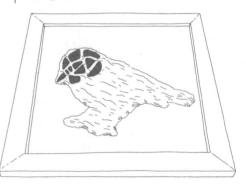

5 Arrange the broken pieces of tile or pottery in the bed of mastic to form the design, leaving ⅛″ to ¼″ between the pieces for grout. Lay mastic around the design and fill in the border with a solid color of tile or pottery. Allow to dry 24 hours.

6 Mix 1–2 cups of grout. Using a spatula or other flat tool, spread the grout into the cracks of the mosaic. Clean the tiles with a damp sponge and allow to cure for 48 hours.

7 Remove the masking tape from the frame. Cover the mosaic edges with masking tape to protect it. Finish the frame as desired.

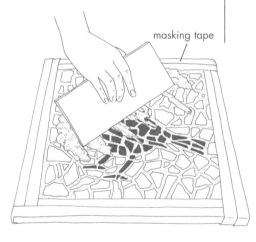

masking tape

SOURCES FOR MOSAIC MATERIAL

Mosaic, an ancient art widely used by the Romans, is the ultimate recycler's art. Tile and flooring stores often have broken, damaged, or remainder tile they will be happy to sell for a very modest price, or even give away. Color selection might be limited, but once the stores know you are looking, they will often happily save scraps for you.

Yard sales are another great source. Old chipped plates in a rainbow of colors abound and can be had for pennies. One Saturday morning on the yard sale circuit should provide supplies for many mosaics to come.

Rooster Tea Cozy

Invite your bird-loving friends over for afternoon tea, and keep your tea warm with this fabric cozy in the shape of a rooster. Enjoy each other's company while you watch the birds outside your window.

MATERIALS

1 yard black-and-white-patterned
   fabric
Scrap of yellow fabric, for beak
One 6″ length of ¾″ red ribbon
Polyester fill
1 package ½″ wide seam binding
3 yards ¼″ ribbon cut in half

EQUIPMENT

Scissors
Needle and thread
Sewing machine
Measuring tape

MAKING THE SPOUT COVER

1 Enlarge the spout and beak patterns on page 111, and transfer onto paper. Cut out fabric, transferring all marks.

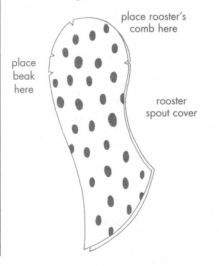

place rooster's
comb here

place
beak
here

rooster
spout cover

2 Sew the beak together on two sides using a scant ¼″ seam. Turn and lightly stuff with polyester fill. Baste closed.

beak

3 To form comb, using a double strand of thread, make a short running stitch along one edge of the red ribbon. Backstitch, and knot at the end. Pull the leading thread,

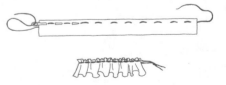

gathering one edge of the ribbon to about a 3″ length, to make the rooster's comb.

4 Place the gathered ribbon on the right side of one of the spout cover pieces between the two marks, with gathering line of ribbon on seam line of spout cover and ribbon width toward center. The gathers should be just inside the cut edge. Baste into place. Baste beak into place. Cover with the other piece of spout fabric, and sew a ½″ seam. Turn the bottom edge under ¼″, and iron. Turn under another ¼″ and sew.

Making the Cozy

5 Measure the teapot to determine the size of the cozy. The cozy should be twice the circumference of the pot's belly and should be the height of the pot plus 3″. Cut the fabric in a rectangle to these dimensions. Fold the fabric in half across the width. Finger press the fold, then open and cut along the crease.

6 Turn the fabric right sides together, matching corners. Measure left end 2″ down from

the top and up from the bottom. Mark and sew from the bottom and top edges to the marks. This will leave an open slit for slipping over the spout. Check to make sure the spout fits through the slit. (You may need to adjust it.) Finish the seams by zigzagging or stitching ⅛″ away from seam and trimming close to the stitching.

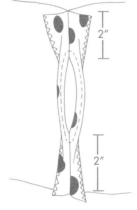

7 Turn edges of the slit under ¼″ and sew. Turn top and bottom edges under ¼″, and press. Turn under again and sew.

8 To make the casing for the drawstring, mark a spot down 1″ from both top corners and up from both bottom corners. Use a yardstick to mark a straight line connecting these marks from end to end. Pin seam binding in place over the marked line, turning under the ends. Baste. Sew close to the edges to make a casing.

9 Run one length of ribbon through each casing. Gather and wrap around the teapot, tying the ribbon at the handle.

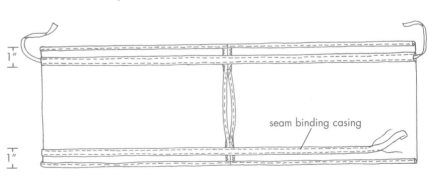

seam binding casing

Bright Flyers Banner

Hang this banner in front of your house to catch the breeze. Bright colors welcome friends to your home. Choose bird and birdhouse motifs on pages 109–115 to create your design.

MATERIALS

Purchased banner or 20″ x 16″ fabric
Scraps of fabric, for the design
½ yard 2-sided fusible web
Dimensional paint or embroidery
  floss

EQUIPMENT

Needle and thread or sewing
  machine
Scissors
Iron
Ironing board
Paint brush or embroidery needle
Cord for hanging

1 To make the banner, turn under the top, bottom, and one side of your fabric ½″ twice. Iron, then sew with a straight stitch. To sew a casing on the fourth side, turn the edge under ½″ and then 1″ and sew close to the edge.

2 Fuse the web to the back of the fabric you will be using for the design. Draw the design on the web's paper backing. (Remember to reverse the

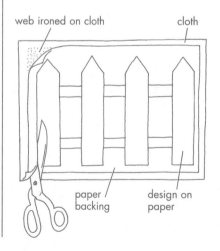

web ironed on cloth · cloth

paper backing · design on paper

design; otherwise, you end up with a mirror image.) Cut out the design and remove the paper backing.

3 Starting with the background pieces, fuse the web-backed design pieces into place following the manufacturer's directions. Layer the design where needed rather than try to butt the pieces together. Continue to fuse each layer of the design.

4 To finish the edges of the fused-on appliqué you can use either dimensional paint or a blanket stitch with embroidery floss. Thread cord through casing and tie to flagpole.

Nesting Bird Ornaments

Folklore holds that having a pair of nesting birds brings good luck. Whether or not they change your fortunes, adding these pretty ornaments to the branches of your holiday tree will create a beautiful, woodsy look. Tie one to a gift wrapped in feather-printed paper for a special occasion.

MATERIALS

Craft bird
Purchased nest
3 small silk flowers
Tacky glue or glue gun
1 sprig baby's breath
10″ of ¼″ ribbon
10″ 18 gauge florist's wire

1 Glue the bird into the bowl of the nest. Tuck the flowers around the bird, securing with glue.

2 Fill in holes around flowers and bird with the baby's breath.

3 Make a bow from the ribbon and place it behind the bird, tucking it slightly underneath.

4 Use the florist's wire to secure to tree.

Nest Building Materials ❧

Find or make a pretty box or bag (see page 22), and start collecting nesting materials. In early spring, birds search out twigs, pine needles, hair, string and yarn, fabric strips, straw, and other building materials to help in nest construction.

Give the box to a friend to set out in a shallow tray or basket for the neighborhood birds to find. This simple gift, an ideal project for a child to tackle, will provide hours of spring birdwatching pleasure.

Quilted Ornaments

These old-fashioned ornaments will be a delight on any tree at the holidays. Rolled up and tied with a ribbon, they're a terrific addition to a festive gift basket. To use them as gift tags, address them with permanent fabric markers.

MATERIALS

White or off-white cotton fabric
Scraps of cotton fabric, for birds and
  birdhouse designs
⅛ yard 2-sided fusible web
Cotton fabric, cut into 2″ strips, for
  the edging
Cotton batting
Quilting thread
8″ length of ⅛″ ribbon, one piece for
  each ornament

EQUIPMENT

Scissors
Sewing machine
Iron
Ironing board

1 Cut two 3″ x 4″ pieces of cotton fabric for the base of the appliqué and for backing. Cut a piece of batting to measure 3″ x 4″.

2 Fuse the web to the back of the fabric that will be used for the designs. Draw the design on the paper backing (see patterns on next page). Cut out the appliqué and fuse it to a piece of cotton base.

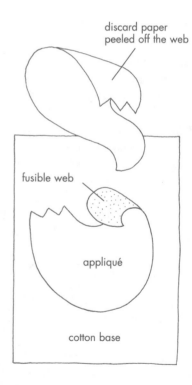

discard paper
peeled off the web

fusible web

appliqué

cotton base

3 Layer the appliquéd piece, batting, and backing, with wrong sides facing batting. Baste together along the edges.

4 Fold the edging lengthwise, wrong sides together, and press. To finish the top and bottom, put the raw edges of the edging along the seam line of the right side of the appliqué and sew a scant ¼″ seam allowance. Turn the edging to the back and slip-stitch in place.

5 Machine- or handstitch around the inside of the appliqué and edgings at ⅛″.

6 Use an 8″ piece of ⅛″ ribbon to make a hanging loop. Sew the ends of ribbon to the back side of the ornament, near the top edge.

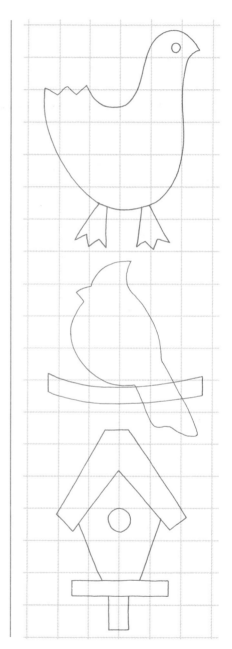

1 square = 1/2″

Tin Holiday Ornaments

Put these sparkling ornaments on your tree and enjoy them for many years to come, or hang them from your porch ceiling by ribbons each 2" different in length. Summer breezes will turn a trio of birds into wind chimes. Made from recycled tin cans, these ornaments are inexpensive.

MATERIALS

Sheet tin from cans, flattened (see pages 102–103 for technique)
Ribbon for hanging

EQUIPMENT

Grease pencil or nail
Tin snips or strong shears
File or emery cloth
Drill
Small round file

1 Copy the bird patterns on page 112. Trace the design to a piece of flattened tin with a grease pencil or nail.

2 Cut out the tin shape using tin snips or shears. Smooth the edges with a file or emery cloth.

3 Drill a hole for hanging. Smooth the edges of the hole with a small round file and tie a ribbon loop for hanging.

CHAPTER 5

Gifts for the Junior Birder

The feather, whence the pen

Was shaped that traced the lives of these good men,

Dropped from an angel's wing.

— William Wordsworth (1770–1850), *Ecclesiastical Sonnets*

It's never too early to get children involved with birds and nature. Their enthusiasm for new things will add to your own enjoyment of the out-of-doors. I love to sit with my children and watch the never-ending show at the birdfeeder.

Nature-Printed T-Shirt

Kids love to wear clothes they've decorated. Let them personalize this shirt with nature-printed feathers, creating designs on their own. Then turn them loose with jeans, sneakers, and baseball caps.

MATERIALS

T-shirt
Cardboard
Assorted feathers
Stamp pad with fabric ink
Scrap paper, several pieces
Tweezers

1 Wash and dry T-shirt to remove sizing. Place a piece of cardboard inside the shirt to prevent the ink from bleeding through to the back.

2 Ink the pad with the fabric ink. You can use basic black, iridescent, or even some of the embossing inks. Get funky and have fun.

3 Lay a feather on the ink pad and cover it with a scrap of paper. Gently press the feather into the ink pad. Make sure you have good coverage of ink on the feather. You can experiment with this technique on a scrap piece of paper to make sure the

feather prints well. When you are done, use the scrap paper as a note card for gift giving!

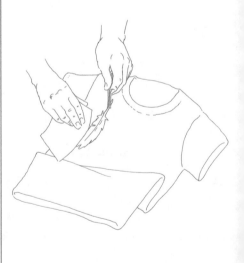

4 Using the tweezers, remove the feather from the ink pad. Lay the feather, inked side down, on the T-shirt and cover with a clean piece of paper. Very gently rub the feather to transfer the ink to the shirt, taking care not to move the feather.

5 Lift the paper and with the tweezers remove the feather from the T-shirt. Let the ink dry, and fix according to the ink manufacturer's instructions. If you've used a water-based ink, the feather can be washed and saved to use again.

VARIATIONS

∾ Make an all-over pattern with the feathers.

∾ Use feathers to accent the neckline, hem, or sleeves.

∾ Use fabric marking pens or water-thinned acrylic paint instead of a fabric ink pad. (Just make sure that the medium you use is washable, so it will withstand the rigors of playing and laundering.)

Do-It-Yourself Easter Egg Dyes ∾

Chop 1 pound of fresh spinach into 3″ pieces. Place the spinach in a pot with 4 cups of water. Simmer for 1 hour, then strain out the leaves, reserving the liquid. Add 4 teaspoons of white vinegar to the spinach water. Add the eggs and simmer in the dye for about 30 minutes.

For other colors, experiment with shredded red cabbage, marigold or dandelion flowers, carrot tops, beets, and tea bags.

The Chicken or the Egg? ∾

The egg came first! The first eggs with shells were laid by reptiles around 280 million years ago. The tough, leathery shells kept the tiny embryonic reptiles safe. Real birds didn't come onto the scene until about 150 million years ago. The reptile eggs had a 130-million-year jump on the ancestor of the barnyard chicken.

Polymer Clay Necklace

Kids delight in creating jewelry for themselves
and friends. This easy polymer clay
necklace is beautiful and a snap to make.
You may have a hard time getting them to quit once they get started.

MATERIALS

Polymer clay
6 large-holed purchased beads
22″ rattail cord

EQUIPMENT

Knitting needle or stiff wire

1 Condition the clay (see pages 104–105 for the technique).

2 To make four polymer clay beads, begin by making four balls about ¾″ in diameter. Elongate slightly. Use a large knitting needle or stiff wire to pierce each one for stringing. The holes will shrink slightly when baked, so make them larger than you think is necessary.

3 To make the polymer clay feather, roll a ball of clay that is slightly more than 1″ in diameter. Elongate and flatten the ball so that it is about ¼″ thick and 2″ long. Make the feather's shaft by forming a cylinder of clay about 3″ long and less than ¼″ wide. Taper one end of the cylinder and lay it on top of the feather body. Press it into the feather. (The quill end will extend over the edge of the feather.)

4 Form a loop at the end of the quill for stringing the feather by rolling the end of the quill toward the back. Cut the shaft to fit and secure the end to the back of the feather by pressing gently. Use a knitting needle or other sharp item to score the front of the feather to simulate the veins.

5 Bake the feather and beads according to the manufacturer's directions. You may need to place the beads on a holder of stiff wire to keep them from flattening during baking.

6 To assemble the necklace, string the feather on the rattail cord and alternate the clay beads and purchased beads to either side. Make a knot in the cord after the last bead. Close the necklace by making a knot.

Speedsters ∽

The smooth, aerodynamic shape of a bird's body and wings, which makes flight possible, also makes birds *fast*. Cars on the highway usually go 55-65 miles an hour. Most flapping birds can go over 100 miles an hour. Swifts, as you can guess from their name, are some of the world's fastest birds. They can reach speeds of up to 200 miles an hour in level flight. And peregrine falcons, who hunt by diving from above onto other birds, can reach speeds of 200 miles an hour during this dinner dive.

Bird Puppet

Puppets have universal appeal. They're fun to use or watch. Make several and stage your own puppet show. Get creative and decorate with feathers and sequins. (Not appropriate for children under three years of age.)

MATERIALS

2 pieces of felt 7″ x 9″, any color
2 pieces of red felt 7″ x 4″
2 pieces of yellow felt 7″ x 4″
Scrap felt for eyes
Feathers, beads, lace, braid, and other trim to decorate puppet
White glue

EQUIPMENT

Scissors
Sewing machine

Note: Seam allowances are ½″.

1 Enlarge the pattern pieces shown on page 113 and transfer to paper. Cut out the felt pieces.

2 Make beak by sewing one red piece to a yellow piece, using a ¼″ seam along two sides as shown. Repeat.

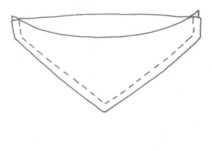

3 Place the two sewn sections of the beak so that the red sides are together. Sew along the top free edge of the red felt pieces, making sure to keep the yellow pieces free.

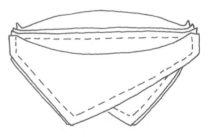

4 Place the bill on the front top piece. Sew along one edge of the yellow side of the beak, keeping the red seamed piece free.

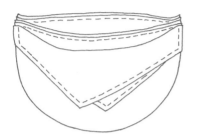

5 Turn over and repeat for the front bottom piece.

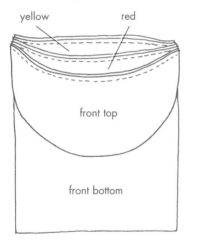

6 Press front top up and beak pieces down.

7 Lay right side of back against right side of front, with beak pieces sandwiched in between. Sew around sides and top, leaving bottom edge open; take a ¼" seam.

8 Clip the seam allowance along the curved top and turn.

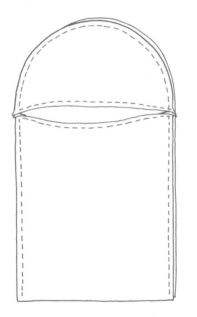

9 Cut ovals 1" long out of scrap felt and glue them on for eyes. Decorate with feathers, beads, sequins, and/or other trimmings. Attach trimmings with glue.

High-Flying Kite

There's nothing so beautiful as a sprightly kite dancing in the wind. Any child will love to make his own and send it soaring. Color with brilliant paints to send his creative dreams soaring.

MATERIALS

White sheet plastic or garbage bag
Permanent marking pens
Two ¼″ dowels, 16″ long
Clear plastic packing tape
Kite string
Fabric scraps or crepe paper for tails

EQUIPMENT

Scissors
Hole punch

1 Cut the plastic to an 11½″ square.

2 With the permanent markers, draw your favorite bird on the plastic or use the bird pattern on page 114. Make it big so that you can see it when the kite is flying.

3 Lay the dowels on the back of the plastic to form a cross from corner to corner.

4 Tape the length of the dowels and reinforce the corners with extra tape.

5 Reinforce the grip of the horizontal dowel with several short pieces of tape placed about 2″–3″ in from each end. Punch

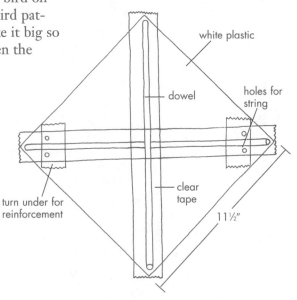

white plastic
dowel
holes for string
clear tape
turn under for reinforcement
11½″

holes on both sides of the horizontal dowel through the reinforcing tape.

6 Cut a 32″ length of kite string. Tie each end of the string to one end of the horizontal dowel through the punched holes. Tie a loop in the center of this string and attach it to the flying string.

7 Make the kite tail out of strips of fabric or crepe paper, and attach with tape to one end of the vertical dowel.

8 Set sail on a windy day.

How Do Birds Fly? ∾

Birds and kites stay in the air for the same reason: lift. In the case of birds and airplanes, the shape of the wing, which is longer and curved on the top and shorter and straighter on the bottom, holds the secret to flight. Air flowing over the wing flows faster over the top because it is longer. This increased speed causes slightly less air pressure above than below the wing. The higher air pressure below pushes the bird up.

The same principle applies to kites. Air flowing against the face of the kite from a breeze (or from running) causes air pressure to build below the kite, which rises against this pressure.

Quill Feather Pen

In times past, writing quills were made from the barnyard goose, but any large feather should do. You might try a feather from a turkey, crow, swan, or seagull. This would make a nice, inexpensive gift — with a bottle of ink — for a child's teacher or scout leader.

MATERIALS

Large feather with a stiff quill
Sharp knife
Piece of wood or cutting board
India ink

1 Remove enough of the soft, feathery part from the writing end to make room for fingers to hold the quill. Use a sharp knife to make a curving cut at the tip. (Children will need an adult helper for this step.)

2 Holding the writing tip flat on a board, make a small, ¼″ slice up the center of the quill for an ink reservoir.

3 Use India ink to write your name. Dip just the very end of the quill into the ink.

Bird Picture from Seed

Use the geese design shown here, or photocopy a bird picture and glue it to poster board. Let your imagination discover birds of a different feather.

MATERIALS

Permanent marker

Stiff poster board

White glue

Several different types of seed
(sunflower, carrot, radish,
pumpkin, for example)

Small piece of cardboard for
squeegee

Tweezers

1 Using permanent marker, make an outline of a bird on poster board (or paste a large picture of a bird on the poster board).

2 Spread white glue in one section of your design. Use a small piece of cardboard as a squeegee to ensure that you get a smooth, even coating of glue.

3 Sprinkle one kind of seed on the glue-covered section. Keep tweezers handy for plucking out unruly seeds.

4 Repeat steps 2 and 3 for each different type and color of seed until your design is complete.

5 Let dry.

VARIATIONS:

- ∾ Use larger seeds if you're working with young children. Chunky seeds will be easier for their small fingers to manage.

- ∾ Dye lighter colored seeds using food coloring.

Pipe Cleaner Bird Mobile

The constant motion of the birds will entertain children of all ages. (Do not use where children younger than three years of age can reach it.)

MATERIALS

5 fluffy feathers about 4″ long
5 chenille pipe cleaners the same color as the feathers
10 wiggly eyes
Yellow plastic fork
White glue
Fishing line (about 3′)
¼″ wooden dowels, one cut to 12″ and two cut to 4″

1 Roll one end of a pipe cleaner into a fiddlehead shape, which will be the bird's head.

2 Bend the remaining length of pipe cleaner back to form a base for the feather tail.

3 Glue the feather to the base created in step 2. The feather should curve up slightly and the quill should be at the head end of the bird.

4 Repeat with remaining pipe cleaners and feathers.

5 Break off the fork tines ¾ inch from the tip and glue one to each of the fiddleheads for beaks. Glue an eye to each side of the head.

6 Tie a 12″ length of fishing line through the top coil of each bird head.

7 Assemble the mobile following the diagram below. Put a small drop of glue on each of the knots.

8 Hang where the breeze will keep your mobile in motion!

Foam Core Birds

MATERIALS

Five 4-color photocopies of birds, about 2″–4″ tall

White glue

Foam core

Stiff wire

Fishing line (about 3′)

¼″ wooden dowels, one cut to 12″ and two cut to 4″

EQUIPMENT

X-acto knife

Needle-nose pliers

Handsaw

1 Cut out the birds. Use white glue to affix the photocopies to the foam core. With an X-acto knife, cut around the birds. If you have a color scanner and printer, you can make mirror images of the birds and glue to the back side of the foam core. Or, glue brightly colored patterned paper to the other side.

2 Cut wire into 2″ lengths. Turn one end of each length with needle-nose pliers to make a loop. Place a drop of glue onto the other end of the wire and push into the foam core at the top of the birds. Let dry while you construct the mobile.

3 Tie a 12″ length of fishing line through the wire loop at the top of each bird.

4 Assemble the mobile, following the diagram for the pipe cleaner bird mobile. Put a small drop of glue on each knot.

Birdie Bath Soap

Kids love water and bubbles and splashing around in the tub. Make these bird-shaped soaps and give them as gifts. Get your kids to help. Either way it's good clean fun.

MATERIALS

3 bars of glycerin soap
3 bars of Ivory soap

EQUIPMENT

Bird-shaped candy molds or cookie
  cutters
Double boiler

1 Melt the glycerin soap in the double boiler. Shave the bars of Ivory into the melted glycerin bars. Stir until the Ivory is melted.

2 Let cool slightly.

3 *If using molds,* pour liquid into them. Allow to cool, and then remove from mold.

If using cookie cutters, pour into a shoebox lid or other shallow box and allow to cool until firm. Use the cookie cutter to cut out the shapes.

VARIATIONS:

◌ Grate one or two bars of soap. Put the mixture into a jar and just cover it with warm water. Let stand until the water dissolves the soap flakes. Put a teaspoon or two into your bath for sudsy fun.

◌ Melt one of the bars of glycerin soap. Cut the remaining soap into ½–¾–inch–square chunks. Stir into the melted glycerin soap until the chunks just begin to melt. Set aside until cool enough to handle. Put into molds. If you wait just a bit longer until the soap begins to harden, you can even sculpt the soap, if you wish.

CHAPTER 6

Personal Gifts for the Bird Lover

*H*ark! hark! the lark at heaven's gate sings,

And Phoebus 'gins arise,

His steeds to water at those springs

On chalic'ed flowers that lies;

And winking Mary-buds begin

To ope their golden eyes:

With everything that pretty is,

My lady sweet, arise.

— William Shakespeare, *Cymbeline*

Hair Clip

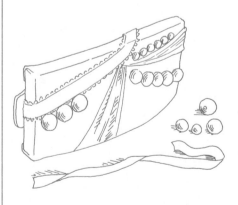

Feathers, fabric, and beads make a beautiful barrette. Try different colors and textures to make each one unique. Barrettes are great hits at bazaars and craft shows. Try your hand at making a variety of styles.

MATERIALS

Plastic barrette blank
White glue
Small pieces of flannel and felt
Fabric scraps, bright colors and
   patterns
Assorted beads, braids, and feathers
Metal barrette or hair clip

EQUIPMENT

Hot glue gun and glue sticks
Bead needle and nylon thread

1 Spread the barrette blank with white glue and cover with flannel. Trim it ¼″ past the edge of the blank. Turn the flannel under and tack down with glue.

2 Place the fabric over the flannel and tack under the edges on the back side with glue. Trim with braid and beads. You can use the glue gun or sew the trim in place.

3 Thread a bead needle with a 20″ length of nylon thread. Tie a knot in the end, leaving a short tail. Push the needle through the fabric, pulling slightly to hide the knot. Put two or three beads on the thread, then pierce the end of a feather with the needle. Run the needle back through the beads and into the fabric and pull taut. This should bring the end of the feather snugly into the beads.

4 Tie off the thread. Place a very small touch of white glue on the knot to keep it tight. Continue with beads and feathers until you are satisfied with the design.

5 Cut a piece of felt slightly smaller than the barrette blank and cover the raw edges on the back.

6 Glue the metal barrette to the back of the blank with the glue gun.

VARIATION

18 inches black rattail cord
White glue
6 peacock feather eyes
3 black pony beads
Plastic barrette blank
One 1-inch black glass cabochon
  stone
Metal barrette or hair clip
Hot glue gun and glue sticks

1 Cut the rattail cord into three even lengths. Dip one end in the white glue and place the quill of a peacock feather eye in the glued cord. Do this to all three pieces of cord. Allow to dry.

2 Using a toothpick, dab a bit of glue at the joint of the cord and feather. String one pony bead on the cord and draw down until it covers the glue. Allow to dry.

3 Cover the barrette blank with white glue. Place the free end of each cord in the glue, so that they hang down. Press the last three peacock feather eyes into the glued cords so that their quills meet in the center.

4 Put a small amount of white glue over the junction of the quills and press the cabochon glass into the glue. Allow to dry completely.

5 Use the glue gun to attach the metal hair clip to the back of the barrette blank.

Polymer Clay Bird Pin

This gift uses the photocopy machine to make a charming, old-fashioned pin. Use a picture from a bird guide book or, for a delightful look, a child's drawing. The photocopy transfers the design to the clay. Experiment with this inventive technique.

MATERIALS

Polymer clay, 1 light color, 2 other
  colors
Black-and-white photocopy of a
  bird, or bird drawing about 2″ wide
Super-bonding glue
Pin backing

1 Condition the polymer clay by rolling it in your hands until it is soft and pliable.

2 To make the "jelly rolls" for the pin's border, start with two colors of polymer clay. From each, make a ball about 1½″ in diameter. Handle each one separately, washing your hands before working with a different color. Take one polymer clay ball and roll it out into a sheet, about 2″ x 6″. Repeat with the second color.

3 Lay one sheet on top of the other. Roll up the two sheets, starting at the long side. Without distorting the layers of color, make sure that the two colors meld together leaving no gaps.

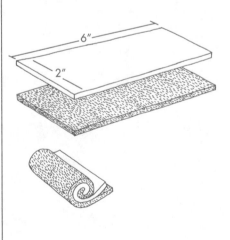

4 Use a thin, sharp blade to slice off pieces ⅛″–¼″ thick. Make enough of these to form a border around a 1½-inch square. Set them aside for a moment.

5 To make the image, flatten a 1½″ ball of white or light-colored clay to about ¼″ thick.

6 Cut around the photocopy of the bird and place it face down on the clay, pressing it firmly in place. You can use a rolling pin or straight-sided bottle to ensure good contact between the clay and your picture.

7 Wait 15 minutes for the picture to transfer. Peel back a very small section to check on the transfer. Remove the paper when you are satisfied with the image.

8 Place the jelly roll slices around the picture, framing it.

9 Bake according to manufacturer's directions. Glue to the pin backing.

Bolo Tie

MATERIALS

Finished polymer design from
  Polymer Clay Bird Pin project
Bolo tie findings
Super-bonding glue
Several feathers
Perle cotton

EQUIPMENT

Glue gun and glue sticks or silicone
  glue

1 Make the polymer clay design following the instructions for making the polymer clay bird pin and glue it to the bolo findings.

2 Remove the metal tips at the ends of the bolo cord. They should come off easily, or snip them off. Glue feathers to the tips of the bolo. Wrap with the perle cotton to cover the quills of the feathers.

3 Wear proudly.

Origami Crane Jewelry

Use bright origami paper to make these stunning pieces of jewelry. Once you learn how to fold cranes, you'll soon have a flock. Challenge yourself to see just how small you can make one.

MATERIALS

Origami paper
Clear lacquer spray
Jewelry findings
  Earrings, post, loop, or clip-on
  Necklace chain with clasp
  Barrette backing
Eye pins
Jump rings
Super-bonding glue

EQUIPMENT

Jeweler's pliers
Glue gun and sticks

Earrings

Make two finished cranes, each about 1″ high.

1 Starting with a 2″-square piece of paper, fold the two cranes (see pages 105–107 for technique).

2 *For loop earrings*, from the bottom, pierce vertically through the body with a needle, making a small hole in the top of the body. Run an eye pin up through the body straight end first, so that the eye is embedded in the body. Use a pin to dab super-bonding glue around the eye pin. Do this to both cranes. Let dry.

eye pin

3 Spray earrings with several light coats of lacquer. Build up these coats slowly, allowing each to dry thoroughly before applying another.

4 Using a jeweler's pliers, make a loop at the top of the pin and connect to loop earring finding with a jump ring. Use a spot of super-bonding glue to close the jump ring and loop at the top of the pin.

loop finding

jump ring

VARIATION

If you are using post or clip-on earring findings, place super-bonding glue on the flat outer face and position bird on it. Be sure to position birds so that they face in opposite directions when worn.

Spray earrings with lacquer as described in step 3.

Necklace

Make three cranes, each about 1″ tall.

1 Follow steps 1–3 for the earrings.

2 Make a loop at the top of each eye pin and attach to the necklace chain with a jump ring. Place one crane at the center of the chain and one to either side. Space them according to their size, so that their wings don't touch.

Barrette

Make three cranes, each with a wingspan of about 2″.

1 Starting with a 2″-square piece of paper, fold three cranes (see pages 105–107 for technique).

2 Using a glue gun, prepare the barrette backing with a bed of glue. Glue the cranes to the backing, aligning them slightly on the diagonal. Their wings should nestle into each other and cover the backing from sight.

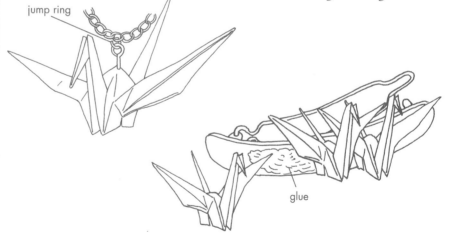

jump ring

glue

Birdseed Paper

There is a certain satisfaction in making so basic an item as paper. Use this paper for note cards, gift tags, and wrapping gifts. Handmade paper has a soft feel and is so easy to make. You can make your paper by recycling almost any paper product: computer paper, wrapping paper, and artist's paper all make excellent handmade papers.

MATERIALS

Used paper
Water
Birdseed

EQUIPMENT

Electric blender
Bucket
Wooden spoon
½-gallon jug
Funnel
Felt or thick woolen fabric
Cookie sheet
Frame, picture or embroidery
Sponge
Rolling pin

MAKING THE PAPER PULP

1 Tear paper into small pieces about 1″ square. Soak overnight in a bucket of water.

2 Macerate the soaked paper pieces in an electric blender or food processor in the ratio of a small handful of paper to 2 cups of water. Blend for only 15–30 seconds. Don't overmacerate or the fibers won't bind properly.

Each blenderful of macerated pulp should make 1 sheet of paper. Make enough pulp for several sheets of paper. Put the pulp in a bucket as you make it.

3 Add 1 tablespoon of seed for each sheet of paper.

MAKING A SHEET OF PAPER

4 You will need a workspace that can handle getting wet. Lay a piece of felt or thick woolen fabric in a cookie sheet or on a thick sheaf of newspaper. Put your frame or embroidery hoop down on the felt.

5 Using a funnel, fill a half-gallon jug with prepared pulp. Pour the pulp into the frame, a scant ⅛″ thick. It's important to do this quickly and smoothly. Shake the cookie sheet or newspaper back and forth and front to back in order to disperse the pulp evenly.

6 Use the sponge to soak up any excess water that escapes the frame. Let the pulp sit for about 1 minute. Carefully remove the frame and place a piece of dry felt over the sheet of pulp. Press gently with the palm of your hand. Then use the sponge to press the excess water from the felt and sheet of paper. Keep wringing the water from the sponge and pressing the water from the felt until most of the excess water is gone.

7 Slowly roll a rolling pin over the top felt. When no more water is coming out of the felt, carefully remove the top felt from the lower one.

8 Hang the sheet of paper — still on the felt — to dry.

9 Proceed with the rest of the pulp to make more sheets of seed paper.

empty frame

paper

cookie sheet

frame

felt

pulp

Note Cards

Send these note cards to bird-loving friends to mark special days. Package several together with envelopes and tie them with a ribbon, and you have a lovely, useful gift.

MATERIALS

Sheet of birdseed paper
  (pages 90–91)
Sheet of paper slightly smaller than
  the birdseed paper
Color photocopy of a bird picture

EQUIPMENT

Hard-leaded pencil
Small paint brush
Glue stick

1 Fold a sheet of birdseed paper in half, matching the short ends. On the front of the note card, lightly draw an oval with a hard-leaded pencil.

2 Dip a small paint brush in water and wet the line. Do this several times until the oval line is saturated. Let it stand for a few minutes to let the water weaken the fibers of the paper. Gently push the oval out. (Use the oval as a gift tag.) ((insert illustration 3544,

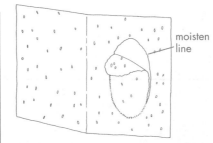

moisten line

3 Cut the color photocopy so that it is slightly smaller than the front of the note card and the bird shows in the oval window. Dab the glue stick on the photocopy and attach it inside the front of the note card.

4 Fold the second sheet of paper and slip it inside the note card. Tack it to the note card with the glue stick.

Seeded Bird Sponge

MATERIALS

Used paper
Alfalfa seeds
or
Grass seeds

EQUIPMENT

Kitchen sponge
Shallow tray
Water

1 Follow the instructions for making the paper pulp. Before pouring into the tray, add the alfalfa or grass seed.

2 Allow the sheet of paper to dry.

3 Cut the paper and sponge into a bird shape using one of the patterns from this book (see page 109). Or create your own design.

4 Place the sponge in the tray. Put the paper on top of the sponge, matching the edges.

5 Pour a small amount of water into the tray, allowing the water to wick up into the sponge. Make sure to get the paper wet.

6 Place the tray in a sunny spot, and keep adding water to maintain moisture. In a week or two you will have a green grassy bird.
  Note: The sponge should not have any antibacterial chemicals in it. Just a good old basic kitchen sponge will do. Rinse it out well just to make sure that there are no lingering chemicals that would hinder germination.

Binoculars Tie Tack

Every man on your bird-watchers list needs this whimsical miniature binoculars tie tack. Or, make two binoculars and glue them to post earrings for a complete set.

MATERIALS

2 pieces black paper, each 12″ long and 1″ wide at one end, tapering to ¼″

2–3 black bugle beads

Super-bonding glue

Clear sealer finish

Purchased tie tack findings

1 Beginning at the wide end of each piece of paper, roll them into tight cylinders. They should be slightly cone-shaped. Secure the cylinders with a touch of glue.

2 Join the two cylinders by putting a dot of glue just at the widest end. They should be side by side now, with a gap between their narrow ends.

glue

3 Apply several layers of polyurethane, varnish, or other clear finish, allowing to dry thoroughly between coats.

4 Glue the bugle beads so that they provide a bridge between the narrowest ends. Let dry.

bugle beads

5 Glue the miniature binoculars to the tie tack findings.

Picture Frame

Frames are versatile gifts that can be crafted to fit any decor. You can decorate frames many different ways, from decoupage to stenciling. Add a favorite photo and you have the perfect present for any occasion.

MATERIALS

Purchased unfinished wooden frame
Acrylic paints
Purchased wooden bird shapes
Faux finish kit
Buttons

EQUIPMENT

Glue gun

1 Finish the frame according to the manufacturer's directions. Allow to dry.

2 Paint the wooden birds with acrylic paint. Sponge around the edges with a lighter color to give a folksy look. Allow to dry.

3 Using the glue gun, attach the birds and buttons to the frame.

Decoupage Frame

MATERIALS

Purchased wooden frame
Acrylic paint
Color photocopies of birds or wrapping paper with a bird motif
Decoupage medium

You can do this in either of two ways: Cover the frame with two coats of acrylic paint, then cut out small birds and decoupage them on, letting some of the paint show. Or, cover the whole frame with decoupage. For the first version, cover the area where the birds will be with a layer of decoupage medium. Place the birds on the medium, smoothing out any wrinkles or bubbles in the paper. After you have placed all the birds, cover the entire frame with decoupage medium.

Cracked Egg Mosaic

MATERIALS

Purchased unfinished wooden frame

Eggshells, washed and broken into
   small pieces

Acrylic paints

1 bottle thick white glue

EQUIPMENT

Two ½–inch sponge brushes

Paper towels

Clear acrylic spray (optional)

1 Paint the frame with a base coat of a light-colored acrylic paint. Let dry completely.

2 Wash the eggshells and break them into pieces about 1 inch square.

3 Using the sponge brush, coat the painted frame with white glue. Press the eggshell into the glue. The outside of the eggshell should be exposed, and the pieces should lie fairly flat. Don't press so hard that glue squeezes out between the pieces. Continue working around the frame until the whole surface is covered. Allow the glue to dry completely.

4 Place a small amount of the desired color of acrylic paint on your palette. You will be using the "dry brush method" of painting, which requires that you dip the second sponge brush into the paint, taking up an amount of paint, then wipe the brush onto the paper towel, removing most of the paint.

5 Gently rub the sponge brush over the bits of eggshell. Work until you are satisfied with the level of coloration. If you get too much color on the shells, use a bit of paper towel to wipe it off.

6 Use clear acrylic spray to seal the finish, if you like.

Fine-Feathered Frame

MATERIALS

Wooden frame

Acrylic paints

Craft feathers

1 bottle white glue

EQUIPMENT

Two ½–inch sponge brushes

1 Use the sponge brush to coat the frame with acrylic paint. The color should be close to that of the feathers you have chosen. Apply a second coat, if needed. Allow to dry.

2 Cover the frame with white glue, using the second sponge brush.

3 Starting at the bottom of the frame, place the feathers on the glue. Point the quills up. Overlap each row on the one below, much like shingling a roof.

4 Continue until you get to the top of the frame. Use the smallest feathers for the top row.

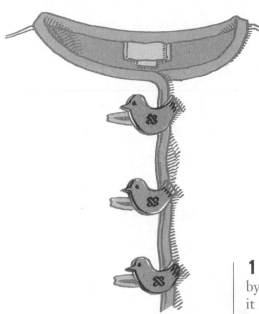

Polymer Clay Buttons

Using these original, handmade buttons is a wonderful way to personalize a piece of clothing. Decorate a plain white shirt with a flock of colorful buttons. Sew buttons to a sweater to personalize your look.

MATERIALS

Polymer clay
Polymer wax or polymer varnish

EQUIPMENT

Glass bottle, or marble rolling pin
Needle and thread
Small, bird-shaped cookie cutter
Juice box straw

1 Condition the polymer clay by rolling it in your hands until it is soft and supple (see page 105). Using a glass bottle or marble rolling pin, roll the clay to a thickness of ⅛″–¼″.

2 Use the cookie cutter to cut out shapes. Smooth the edges with your finger.

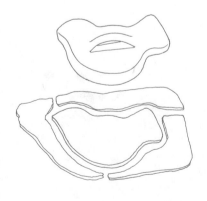

3 With a large needle or small juice box straw, make two holes to sew through. They will shrink a bit when you bake the clay, so make them slightly larger than they need to be for the thread.

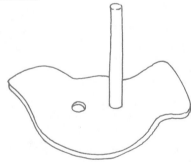

4 Bake the buttons according to the manufacturer's directions. Let cool and remove from baking sheet.

5 Finish with a polymer floor wax, or a varnish made specifically for the polymer clays. Allow the finish to dry thoroughly. Sew to clothing.

Note: Do not use cooking utensils for shaping or baking polymer clay. The clay is made from polyvinyl chloride, the same material that's in your household pipes. So save this bird-shaped cookie cutter just for this purpose. Always remove the buttons before laundering or dry cleaning.

VARIATIONS

ଓ Take an 18-inch length of rattail cord or thin strip of leather, and string it through the buttons. Tie knots on either side of the buttons to hold them in place. Knot the cord and you have a quick and charming necklace.

ଓ Make the button into a pin. When you're making the button, don't make the holes. Bake according to manufacturer's directions. Using the hot glue gun, glue a small pin backing to the backside of the wee birdie.

ଓ Give a gift of cuff links to your favorite bird lover of the French cuff persuasion. Make two bird button covers that are identical. Hot glue them to cuff link findings. Wrap them with feather-printed paper.

ଓ The button covers also make great decorations on candles. You can use purchased candles for this quickie idea. Put the baked button covers in hot water. This will soften them a bit. After they have warmed,

Button Covers ଓ

Follow instructions for bird buttons, but don't make the holes in the bird shapes. Bake according to the clay manufacturer's directions. When the buttons are cool, glue them to button cover findings with a super-bonding glue.

remove them one at a time and dry them on a towel. Use a second candle to drip a few drops of wax on the back of the button covers before sticking them to the decorated candle.

ଓ You can give a plain denim vest or dress a countrified look by sewing birdie buttons on it. Using stout thread, place a few around the neckline. Remove buttons when laundering the garment.

Appliquéd Vest

You can either use a purchased vest or sew one yourself to make this wonderful gift. Either way, it will make a marvelous addition to any wardrobe. Calico creates a casual look that goes with jeans. Use velvets and satins for holiday elegance.

MATERIALS

Purchased or sewn vest
Fabric scraps for the appliqués
2-sided fusible web
Embroidery floss or dimensional
 paint

1 Enlarge patterns on page 115. Fuse the web onto the back of the fabric according to the manufacturer's instructions. Transfer the pattern to the paper backing the fusible web. Remember that this is a mirror image of the finished design.

2 Cut out the design and then remove the paper that backs the web. Iron it to the vest.

3 With embroidery floss, blanket-stitch around the edges, or use the dimensional paint to seal the edges.

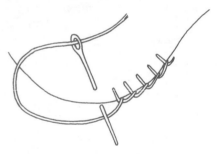

CHAPTER 7

Techniques

*I*n this final section you will find advice, instruction, and tips for carrying out a variety of techniques used to make the projects in this book. Learn them, use them, and then enjoy experimenting with your own new ideas.

MAKING AND USING SUET

Suet seedcakes are made for birds that eat both insects and seeds. These cakes will attract goldfinches, grosbeaks, northern orioles, scarlet tanagers, and woodpeckers. Suet provides much-needed fat and protein in the winter months. The summer suet recipe is particularly favored by tanagers, thrushes, and warblers.

1 Ask your butcher for several pounds of beef suet; the hard white fat from behind the kidneys is best. You can substitute drippings from your kitchen if raw suet is not available.

2 Grind or coarsely chop suet into small pieces. Melt raw suet in double boiler or over low heat in a heavy-bottomed pan. Cool slowly until it hardens. Do not refrigerate.

3 Melt the suet again and let cool slightly. It will be harder after the second melting. Pour over seeds in molds, or empty grapefruit, orange, or coconut shells.

Summer Suet Substitute ∽

Suet can turn rancid in the summer. Try this recipe in the hot months.

1 part flour
3 or 4 parts yellow cornmeal
Dash salt
1 part peanut butter
1 part vegetable shortening

Mix all ingredients and stir. Spoon into molds or fruit rinds and hang outside.

Adapted from *Bird Food Recipes*, by Rhonda Massingham Hart

Additions to Suet
Millet
Sunflower seeds
Raisins
Cornmeal
Cooked oatmeal
Cooked rice
Cracked corn
Chopped peanuts
Cooked noodles
Cooked spaghetti
Bread (dried and ground)
Meat (dried and ground)
Hemp seed
Dried berries

∽ WOODWORKING

For the woodworking projects in this book you'll need an assortment of sandpaper, rulers, and squares. The projects are well within the scope of the weekend woodworker.

Wood and paint. Wood is the ideal building material for nesting boxes and feeders. It's durable, a good insulator, and breathes. Birds are comfortable with the natural feel of wood, especially if it is left unpainted. Birds avoid bright colors; if you decide to paint, stick to darker shades — the birds seem to know that bright colors can attract predators. Don't paint the inside or the entrance hole. An unfinished interior will help nestlings grip the walls of the birdhouse when it's time to try their wings. Many bird species prefer slab wood with the bark still on it.

Avoid using metal for birdhouses. They can heat up like ovens, injuring the occupants.

Ventilation and drainage. Provide ventilation by drilling ¼″ holes under the eaves. Don't forget to allow for drainage by drilling ¼" holes in the floor of the birdhouse or feeder.

To make it last. You can use cedar or other rot-resistant wood, or coat the outside of ply-wood with marine-grade varnish. Use galvanized or brass nails, screws, and hinges to prevent rust. Glue all joints before you nail or screw them together to prolong the life of the birdhouse. Use a waterproof glue or clear silicone.

Use acrylic water-based stain to provide a long-lasting finish. If you use acrylic paint, use a sealer coat of Thompson's Water Seal or Varathane's Natural Oil Finish.

Maintenance. Remember to provide a way to clean out the nesting boxes; most birds won't use an old nest. Hinges or swinging panels will simplify your housekeeping chores.

When you give someone the birdhouses, feeders, or bird-baths, include some simple instructions written on a note card so the recipient knows how to use your gift. This is especially important if your friend is new to birding.

❧
MOSAICS

Mosaics are an elegant way to enliven concrete outdoors or to brighten interior projects. Don't be intimidated by this technique. It's very easy and relatively inexpensive. It's also very durable. Mosaics found in the ruins of Pompeii are evidence of how long they can last.

What you use to make a mosaic is limited only by your imagination. Tile, stone slabs, pebbles, glass nuggets, broken pottery, and tessera are some of the most common materials.

Placing the design. Begin with a rigid surface such as concrete or thick wood. For a large project, lay down a bed of mastic; for small projects, dab a bit of mastic on the back of the tessera or tile and set the pieces onto the surface you wish to decorate.

Grouting. Grout is the fine-grained cement mortar used to fill the cracks once all the tiles have been set in place. You'll find it at ceramic tile supply and hardware stores. To provide a more interesting design, it can be colored, using grout dyes available at ceramic tile supply stores. You'll need a pound of grout for every 2 or 3 square feet of mosaic surface.

To mix grout, place dry grout in a bucket and add water, stirring, until you have a creamy paste. After your tiles are set, apply the grout right over them. Wipe the grout off your mosaic pieces with a damp sponge.

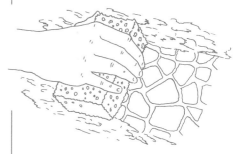

Concrete and Cement

The Romans were the first to use concrete and cement in their buildings. Ancient viaducts and roads made of concrete are still being used. Today, people use concrete in more inventive ways in art and architecture.

The materials. Concrete, cement, and mortar differ in content. *Concrete* is made by mixing cement, sand, gravel, and water. *Mortar* contains cement, sand, and water. *Cement* is a dry mixture of lime, clay, and gypsum. When water is added to cement, a chemical reaction causes it to harden.

You can add aggregate (often gravel) to concrete to make birdbaths that you can leave plain, brush to reveal the aggregate, or decorate with mosaic.

Using concrete. For small jobs, such as the birdbath, you can purchase ready-mixed concrete. However, if you want to mix your own, use these ingredients:

1 part cement
2 parts sand
3 parts gravel

Put these ingredients into a wheelbarrow and stir. Add water to create a "mud" of the right consistency to easily mold. It shouldn't be too runny or too crumbly.

Mortar for mosaics. You can buy dry, ready-mixed mortar or make your own by mixing 1 part Portland cement, 3 parts sand, and enough water to make the mortar workable but not runny. Add a cement bonding adhesive — 2–3 tablespoons to every gallon of water.

Tinworking

You have a nearly inexhaustible and inexpensive source of sheet metal in your kitchen cabinets: canned food tins. The tin is easily worked with simple tools. Master the technique and decorate your home with this Old World technique.

To prepare a tin can for use, start by removing both ends with a can opener. Save these round end pieces for occasions when you need small pieces of tin. Turn the can opener on its side to remove the rims of the can. Cut along the can's seam with tin snips or heavy-duty shears. Be careful to keep the pressure on the cut to prevent ragged edges. Using a rubber mallet, flatten the metal to create a rectangle.

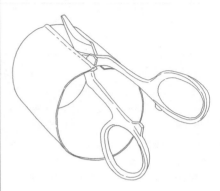

To create designs, use a grease pencil, awl, or sharp nail to mark the metal for cutting. If you are using a pattern, glue it to the tin with rubber cement, which is easily removed. Cut straight lines and wide curves with tin snips; use heavy old scissors for tight curves. Use a jigsaw with a metal cutting blade for inside cuts. Place the tin between two thin pieces of plywood to make your cuts more easily. The plywood will keep the tin from bouncing with the saw.

A nailset can be used for punching holes in the sheet metal. A rigid surface, such as plywood, placed behind the metal, will support it while you punch holes.

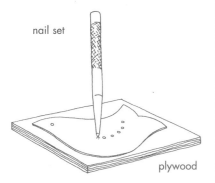

nail set

plywood

Finish your projects by smoothing edges with sandpaper or emery cloth. Polish to a high sheen with steel wool. If desired, apply a coat of metal varnish to protect the bright finish.

If you want to add color, model enamels are perfect — easy to apply, and long lasting.

STENCILING

It's very easy to get excellent results from stenciling. With a bit of preparation, you'll be ready to go. You can purchase stencils or make your own designs. Even if you've never painted before you will be successful with this technique. You'll need:

Stencil polyester film (Mylar)
Sharp knife (X-acto or stencil knife)
Paint
Applicator

Begin by tracing or enlarging patterns or designs as described on page 107, or using a photocopier. Place the Mylar over your design and secure it with tape.

Using the knife, cut out the stencil. Try to keep the lines smooth. (Make a few practice stencils until you feel comfortable with the technique.)

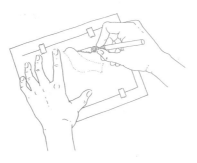

The paint. Choose the type of paint according to the material you'll be stenciling. Both oil-based and acrylic paints can be used on a variety of surfaces. There are artist's stencil paints and crayons formulated especially for this technique. For a good general paint, you can't go

wrong with artist's acrylic. If you are stenciling fabric, however, a fabric stencil paint will get the best results.

How to stencil. Place the stencil on your fabric or other material and secure it with tape. Place a small amount of paint on a palette or tray (a little paint goes a long way in stenciling). Dip a stencil brush or small sponge into your paint. Dab the brush or sponge on a scrap of paper, until the implement is mostly dry. Using a circular scrubbing motion, work from the outside to the center of the design. Carefully lift the stencil to check the design. Apply more paint as needed. It's better to build up layers of paint than to risk getting smudgy results by using too much paint.

PACKAGING AND WRAPPING IDEAS

Making your own wrapping paper and gift bags can be almost as much fun as creating the gift. You can make someone feel very special by taking the time to wrap creatively. Whole books have been written on the subject. Look around for inspiration.

Stamping. One of the simplest ways to customize your wrapping is to use a feather to stamp plain wrapping or butcher paper. You can also use this method on plain gift bags. Decorate gift tags made from handmade paper and tie with bits of raffia. You can also feather print ribbon.

Fabric wraps. Take a scarf that you have made and lay it flat. Place the gift you are giving in the center of the scarf. Draw up the corners and tie with a bit of ribbon. Add a couple of origami cranes as decoration.

Bandboxes make great gift boxes. You can buy them in kit form or ready-made to decorate. Decorating ideas are endless. Paint, stencil, decoupage, or stamp them.

Papier mâché. Inflate a balloon to a size that is just larger than your gift. Cover the balloon in papier mâché. (Or use strips of newsprint dipped in white glue diluted with water.) Let dry. Carefully make a hole in the balloon and let the air out slowly. Remove the balloon or trim around opening. Paint and decorate to your heart's content. Cut the sphere in half, enclose your gift in it, replace halves, and tie with a pretty bow.

Gift baskets. As a gift for someone who is just starting out, place a field guide, birding notebook, and a bottle of insect repellent in a basket. Include a feather-printed note card with some beginning birding tips.

Gift wrap. For a fun and whimsical wrapping paper, stencil plain brown paper with the bird footprints. Kids, especially, will enjoy this design.

Packing material. Use small feathers for packing material; in the spring, they can be set out to provide nesting materials. Use black oil sunflower seeds for packing material around the bird feeders.

POLYMER CLAY

Polymer clay goes by several brand names and is available at craft stores and art supply shops. Fimo and Sculpey are two of the most common. The clay is made up of (PVC) polyvinyl chloride and it comes in many colors. Polymer clay is easily manipulated; even beginners can get great results.

Equipment. One of the advantages of polymer clay is that you don't need a lot of tools. You can adapt many household items to its use. Either your kitchen oven or a small toaster oven is needed to bake the clay. It's important to be able to vent any fumes created by the baking process.

Both the pasta machine and food processor are useful to have around when designing with polymer clay. The pasta machine can roll very uniformly thin sheets of clay. The food processor quickly conditions the clay, a vital step in the process.

But it's important not to use any tool used on the clay in food preparation. The clay is toxic when ingested. So only use food preparation tools dedicated to use with polymer clay.

You will need a smooth, nonporous working surface. Glass, tile, or plastic brayers can be used for rolling and flattening the clay, or you can use a flat-sided glass bottle or a spare rolling pin.

A sharp knife such as an X-acto is essential for making precise cuts. You will also need some kind of needle or awl for making any necessary small holes in the clay before baking it.

Getting started in using polymer clay is as easy as breaking off a chunk and rolling it in your hands to warm it. This is called "conditioning," which is very important in the process. You can warm the clay in many different ways. Just make sure to avoid getting the clay too warm, or you may bake it before you really mean to.

Decoration. After shaping the clay, embellish it with anything that can tolerate being heated at 260°–275°F.

Baking. Polymer clay is baked at a low temperature for up to 2 hours. Each clay has a different formulation and requirements. Make sure to check the labels and use an oven thermometer for accuracy. Don't bake at temperatures higher than 275 degrees.

Finish the clay by buffing it with a soft cloth to bring out the sheen, or apply clear varnish made specifically for polymer clays. You can also use a polymer floor wax applied with a small sponge brush or cotton applicator.

It can be difficult for glue to bond polymer clay to surfaces of things like metal findings. The best bet is to bake the findings right into the clay. The super-bonding glues work well, but experiment with different ones to find out which works best for you.

MAKING ORIGAMI CRANES

Although any square sheet of paper will do for practice, for finished cranes, try to find some origami paper.

Traditional origami paper has one colored side and one white side. It is also very thin but strong, and will not rip easily, which makes it ideal for beginners. If you cannot find origami paper, or if you want to practice before using it, wrapping paper is a good choice because it also has only one decorated side and is thin and relatively inexpensive. But be aware that it does rip easily.

1 Start with a square sheet of paper. With the white side of the paper facing up, crease the paper along both diagonals and both center lines as shown.

2 Turn the paper over so that the colored side is up and the corners face up, down, left and right, or as we will refer to them, north, south, east and west.

Now for the first the next tricky part. Grasp the east and west corners and pull them together underneath the other two points. Holding them, pinch the north and south points together on top of them, as shown. You should end up with a square, oriented like a diamond, with the open end pointing south.

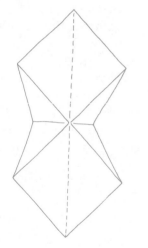

3 In this step you are creating a series of creases, similar to those you made in the first step. These will act as folding guides for upcoming steps. Keeping the closed point to the north, fold the top layer east and west, points in to the center line, as shown. Turn crane over and repeat on the other side. You should have a kite shaped piece of paper. Now fold the north point of the kite down, creating a triangle pointed south.

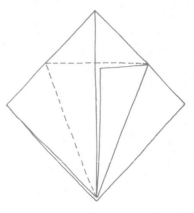

4 Unfold the creases you just made to return your fledgeling crane to the square from step 2.

5 Now for tricky part. Using the creases you just made as a guide, pull the top layer of the southern tip straight up along the top crease. Fold the east and west points in along their creases to form a very tall diamond. Turn over and repeat.

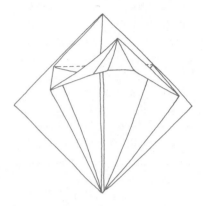

6 Now fold the east and west points in to the center as shown. Turn over and repeat.

7 Great. Now for the last tricky part. Carefully spread apart the western midpoint and grasp the left-hand southern point. Pull it up, reversing the center fold, and flatten. Repeat with the other southern point.

8 To make the head of the crane, gently separate the east point and pull the tip down, reversing the fold, as shown.

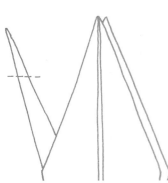

9 Now that your creation actually looks like a crane, you have one easy step left. Gently pull the wings down while blowing into the hole on the bottom of the crane. This will inflate the crane's body and position the wings for flight. Congratulations. Don't worry if your first attempt is not perfect. As you practice, take care in making your folds and creases as exact and clean as possible. Many beginners use a blunt point (like that on a big knitting needle) to score their folds. Experiment to find a working style that suits you, and you'll soon be making beautiful cranes for all your friends.

∾

HOW TO ENLARGE A PATTERN

The patterns on the following pages are overlaid with a grid, and you will need to enlarge them to a specified size. Usually one square equals 1 inch. The easiest way to do this is to use the enlargement/reduction feature on a photocopier. Or as an alternative, draw a grid with 1-inch squares on a piece of paper. Then copy the pattern, square by square, onto your new grid.

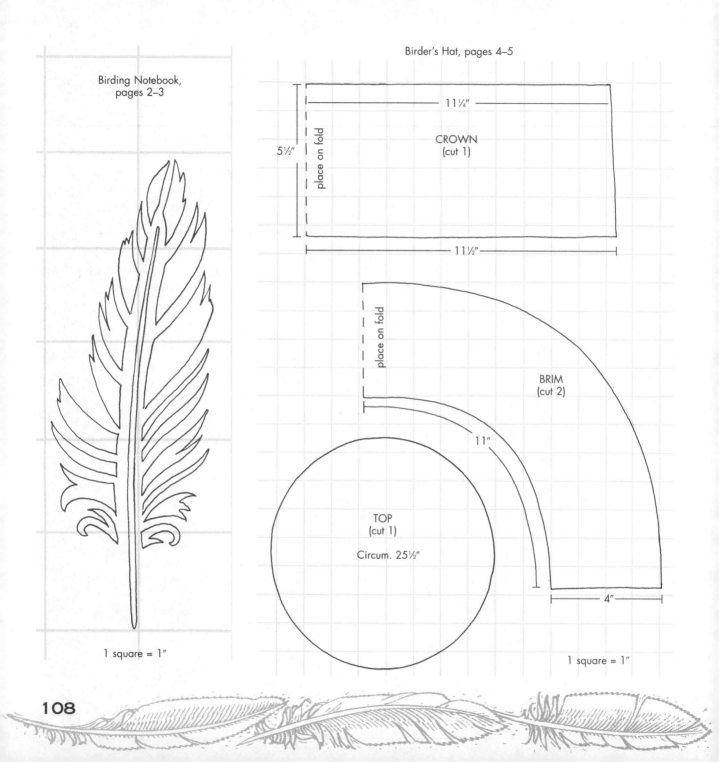

Birding Notebook,
pages 2–3

1 square = 1″

Birder's Hat, pages 4–5

place on fold

5½″

11¼″

CROWN
(cut 1)

11½″

place on fold

BRIM
(cut 2)

11″

TOP
(cut 1)

Circum. 25½″

4″

1 square = 1″

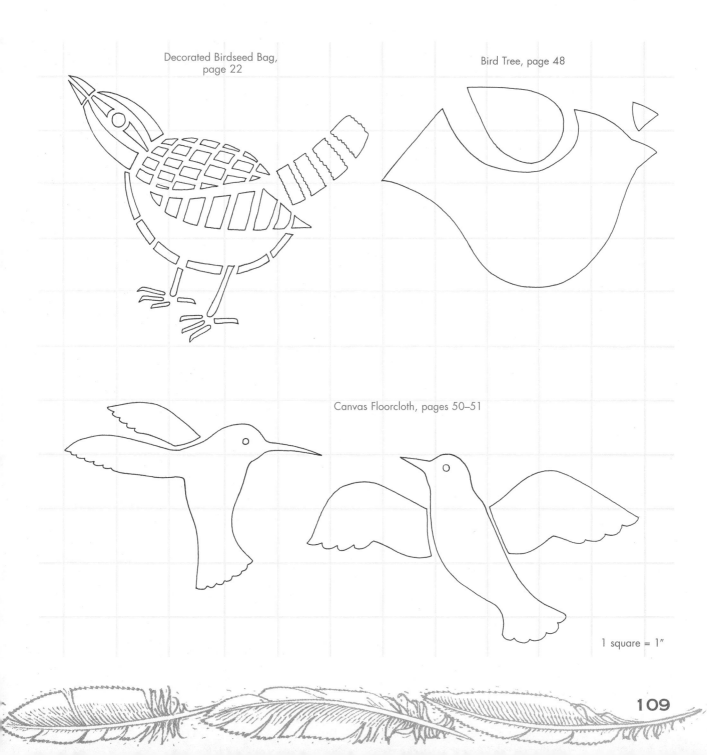

Decorated Birdseed Bag,
page 22

Bird Tree, page 48

Canvas Floorcloth, pages 50–51

1 square = 1"

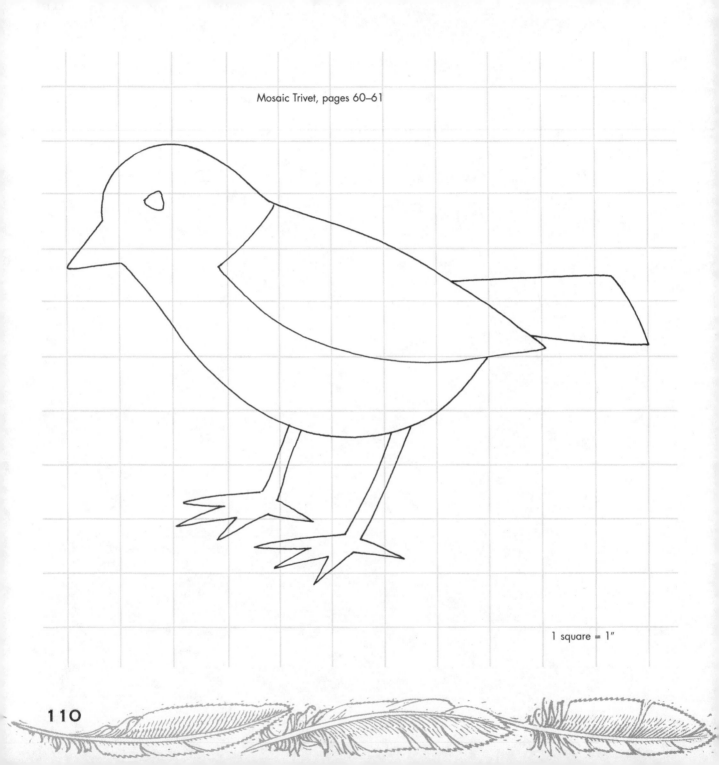

Mosaic Trivet, pages 60–61

1 square = 1″

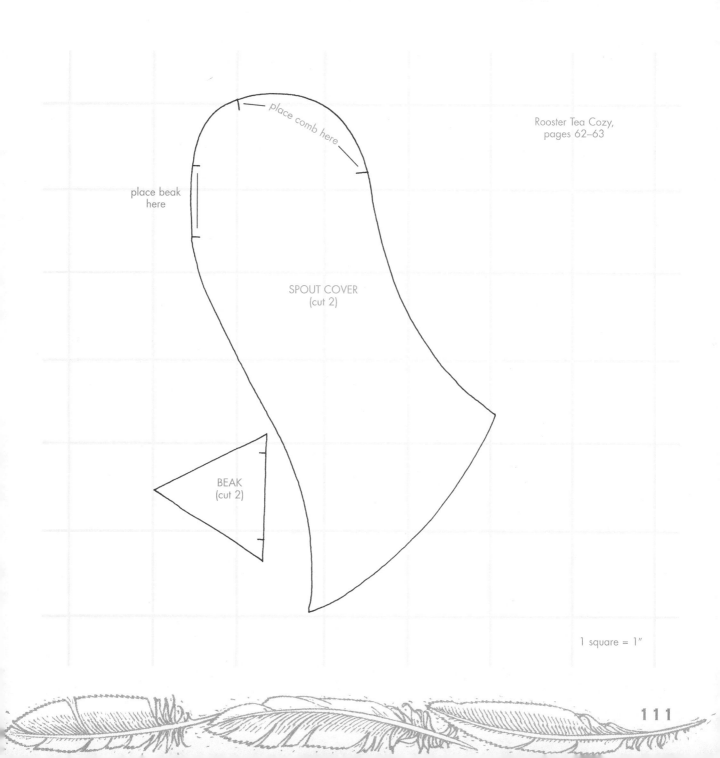

place comb here

place beak
here

SPOUT COVER
(cut 2)

BEAK
(cut 2)

Rooster Tea Cozy,
pages 62–63

1 square = 1″

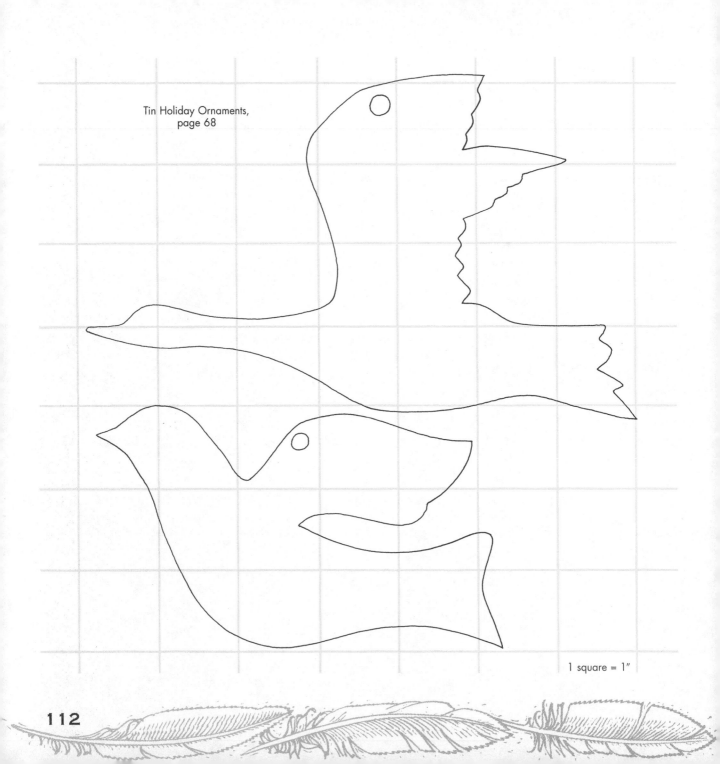

Tin Holiday Ornaments,
page 68

1 square = 1"

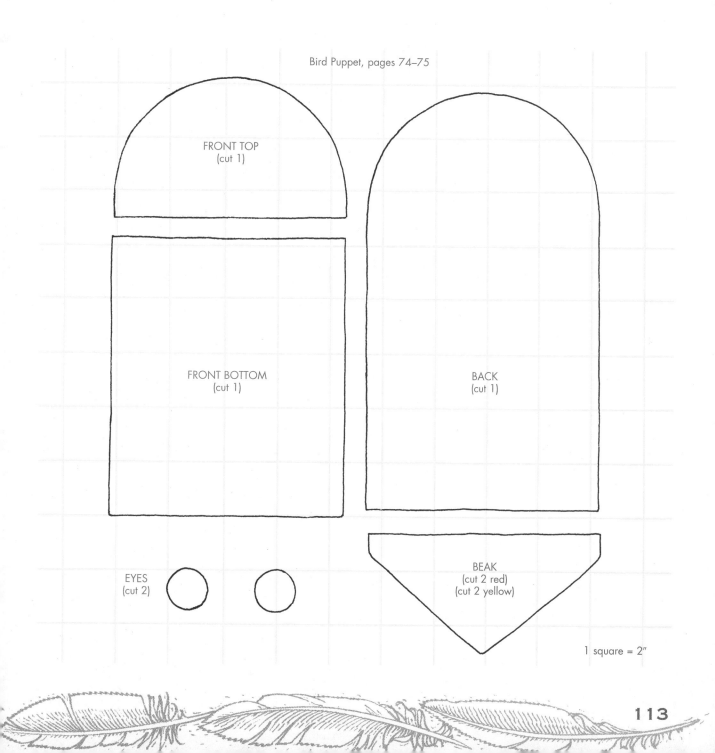

Bird Puppet, pages 74–75

FRONT TOP
(cut 1)

FRONT BOTTOM
(cut 1)

BACK
(cut 1)

BEAK
(cut 2 red)
(cut 2 yellow)

EYES
(cut 2)

1 square = 2"

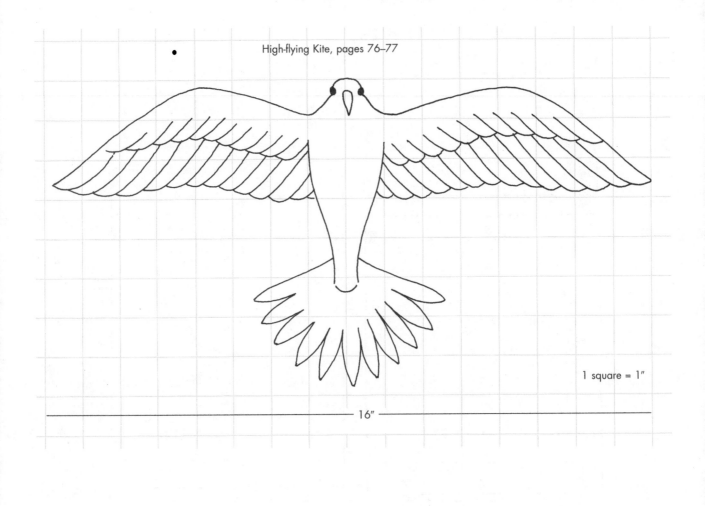

High-flying Kite, pages 76–77

1 square = 1"

16"

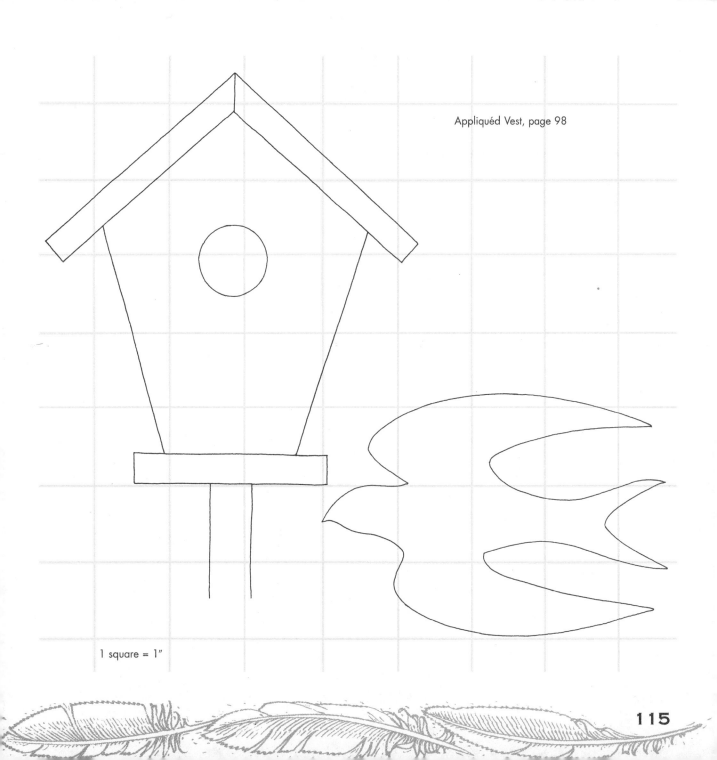

Appliquéd Vest, page 98

1 square = 1"

SOURCES

Seeds Blum
Idaho City Stage
Boise, ID 83706
208-342-0858
*A "Birdseed Garden Seed
Collection"*

Stokes Seeds, Inc.
Box 548
Buffalo, NY 14240
716-695-6980
Birdhouse gourd seeds

W. Atlee Burpee & Co.
300 Park Avenue
Warminster, PA 18974
800-888-1447
Birdhouse gourd seeds

Park Seed Co.
Cokesbury Road
Greenwood, SC 29647-0046
800-845-3369
Birdhouse gourd seeds

Daniel Smith
4150 First Avenue South
P.O. Box 4268
Seattle, WA 98124-5568
1-800-426-6740
*Artist's and printmaking supplies,
papyrus, papers (free catalog)*

Sunshine Discount Crafts
P.O. Box 301
Largo, FL 34649-0301
813-538-2878
*Polymer clay, jewelry findings,
vests, banners, floorcloths, stencils,
stamp supplies*

Enterprise Arts
P.O. Box 2918
Largo, FL 34649
1-800-366-2218
*Jewelry findings, polymer clay,
jeweler's tools*

READING

Baldwin, Edward A. *The Weekend Workshop Collection of Birdfeeders, Shelters, and Baths.* Pownal, VT: Storey Publishing, 1990.

Bethmann, Laura D. *Nature Printing with Herbs, Fruits, and Flowers.* Pownal, VT: Storey Publishing, 1996.

Bull, John, and John Farrand Jr. *The Audubon Society Field Guide to North American Birds*, vol. 1. New York: Alfred A. Knopf, 1977.

Gerrard, Jon M., and Gary R. Bortolotti. *The Bald Eagle: Haunts and Habits of a Wilderness Monarch.* Saskatoon, Canada: Western Producer Prairie Books, 1988.

Godfrey, W. Earl. *The Birds of Canada* (revised edition). Ottawa, Canada: National Museum of Natural History, 1986.

Hart, Rhonda M. *Bird Food Recipes.* Pownal, VT: Storey Publishing, 1995.

Holroyd, Geoffrey, and Howard Coneybeare. *Compact Guide to Birds of the Rockies.* Edmonton, Canada: Lone Pine Publishing.

Peterson, Roger Tory. *A Field Guide to the Birds East of the Rockies.* Boston: Houghton Mifflin Company, 1980.

——. *A Field Guide to Western Birds.* Boston: Houghton Mifflin Company, 1961.

Ramuz, Mark, and Frank Delicata. *Birdhouses: 20 Step-by-Step Woodworking Projects.* Pownal, VT: Storey Publishing, 1996.

Rupp, Rebecca. *Everything You Never Learned about Birds.* Pownal, VT: Storey Publishing, 1995.

Saddington, Marianne. *Making Your Own Paper: An Introduction to Creative Papermaking.* Pownal, VT: Storey Publishing, 1993.

Scott, Shirley L., editor. *A Field Guide to the Birds of North America.* Washington, DC: National Geographic Society, 1983.

Taverner, P. A. *Birds of Canada.* National Museum of Canada, 1934.

——. *Birds of Eastern Canada.* National Museum of Canada, 1919.

——. *Birds of Western Canada.* National Museum of Canada, 1926.

Udvardy, Miklos D.F. *The Audubon Society Field Guide to North American Birds*, vol. 2. New York: Alfred A. Knopf, 1977.

Woodier, Olwen. *Attracting Birds.* Pownal, VT: Storey Publishing, 1981.

INDEX

Page references in *italic* indicate illustrations.

Other Storey Titles You Will Enjoy

The Backyard Bird-Lover's Guide, by Jan Mahnken. For all levels of birders, this book covers feeding, as well as the territory, courtship, nesting, laying, and parenting characteristics of many birds. An identification section is also included, describing 135 species and providing watercolors of each bird. 320 pages. Paperback. ISBN #0-88266-927-3.

Birdfeeders, Shelters & Baths: Over 25 Complete Step-by-Step Projects for the Weekend Woodworker, by Edward A. Baldwin. This book contains designs for a wide range of birdfeeders and baths that will attract birds to your backyard all year. 128 pages. Paperback. ISBN #0-88266-623-1.

Birdhouses: 20 Unique Woodworking Projects for Houses and Feeders, by Mark Ramuz. This book contains designs ranging from classic and simple to whimsical and ornate. It also includes plans with easy-to-follow illustrations, instructions, materials and tools lists, and ideas for how to finish, decorate, and weatherproof the piece. 128 pages. Paperback. ISBN #0-88266-917-6.

Everything You Never Learned about Birds, by Rebecca Rupp. This book is overflowing with amazing facts, fun projects, and fascinating legends about birds. From the first egg-laying dinosaur 280 million years ago to the first known bird 150 million years ago to the modern eagle, this book keeps all ages enthralled. It also includes fun facts such as why ducks don't get wet, how birds got their names, and why birds can tolerate eating worms. 144 pages. Paperback. ISBN #0-88266-345-3.

Gifts for Herb Lovers: Over 50 Projects to Make and Give, by Betty Oppenheimer. This book uses detailed instructions and step-by-step illustrations to help readers make over forty herb-related projects. 128 pages. Paperback. ISBN #0-88266-983-4.

Herbal Treasures: Inspiring Month-by-Month Projects for Gardening, Cooking, and Crafts, by Phyllis V. Shaudys. A compendium of the best herb crafts, recipes, and gardening ideas. 320 pages. Paperback. ISBN #0-88266-618-5.

Making Your Own Paper: An Introduction to Creative Papermaking, by Marianne Saddington. This book contains step-by-step instructions and color illustrations that provide the beginner with information about using a mold, pressing and drying, coloring and texturing, preparing a writing surface, and creating paper art and crafts. 96 pages. Paperback. ISBN #0-88266-784-X.

Nature Printing with Herbs, Fruits, and Flowers, by Laura Donnelly Bethmann. Nature printing is applying paint directly to plants and flowers to press images onto stationery, journals, fabrics, walls, furniture, and more. Step-by-step instructions for collecting specimens, designing artwork, and printing are provided, accompanied by color photos and illustrations. 96 pages. Hardcover. ISBN #0-88266-929-X.

These books and other Storey books are available at your bookstore, farm store, garden center, or directly from Storey Publishing, Schoolhouse Road, Pownal, VT 05261, or by calling 1-800-441-5700. www.storey.com